Dropshipping Made Simple - The Ultimate Guide To Make Money With Shopify And E-Commerce

Adidas Wilson

Published by Adidas Wilson, 2019.

While every precaution has been taken in the preparation of this book, the publisher assumes no responsibility for errors or omissions, or for damages resulting from the use of the information contained herein.

DROPSHIPPING MADE SIMPLE - THE ULTIMATE GUIDE TO MAKE MONEY WITH SHOPIFY AND E-COMMERCE

First edition. May 30, 2019.

Copyright © 2019 Adidas Wilson.

ISBN: 978-1393679493

Written by Adidas Wilson.

Adidas Wilson
P.O. Box 2262
Antioch, Tn. 37011
siriusvisionstudios@gmail.com
www.financierpro.com

Disclaimer

THE AUTHOR HAS MADE every effort to ensure the accuracy of the information within this book was correct at time of publication. The author does not assume and hereby disclaims any liability to any party for any loss, damage, or disruption caused by errors or omissions, whether such errors or omissions result from accident, negligence, or any other cause.

Table of Contents

Introduction

It is safe to assume that since you are reading this, you already have drop shipping fundamentals figured out. If you are serious and want your business to prosper, the following financial and business steps will help. Most entrepreneurs know, including a drop shipping business, require a great deal of commitment. For anyone looking for a quick-rich scheme, drop shipping is not it. You must invest heavily with either money or time. For total newbies in drop shipping, this method is better than investing money because: You get to learn the fundamentals of the business. As it scales and grows, you will be better equipped to manage others. You will know the market and customers at an intimate level and, consequently, make better decisions. You will not fall into the trap of spending money where it is not profitable. You will acquire new skills that will help you as an entrepreneur. You can create a successful drop shipping business by investing a large sum of money. However, this is not the best method. When a business is in its early stages, it is wise to have someone who is invested in its success. Without understanding of the basic functions of your business, you will have to spend outrageous amounts on marketers, programmers, and developers. At the end of the day, you may not make any money. Even though you decide to invest time, you will still require an upfront cost. The most common business structures include: Sole Proprietorship: this business structure is the simplest to implement. However, it does not have personal liability protection. When someone sues your business, your personal assets are not protected. Limited Liability Company (LLC): with this structure, your business is considered a separate entity and your personal assets are protected. The protection is barely maximum, but it is better than a sole proprietorship in this area.

C Corporation: this is the best structure for liability protection. As you can guess, it is not easy to incorporate, and the taxation will be double. Smaller businesses prefer a sole proprietorship or sometimes the LLC. In many cases, the LLC works just fine. All businesses are required by the IRS to have an EIN (employer identification number). It is like the Social Security number of your business. The process of getting one is simple and free. One of the biggest mistakes you can make when starting your business is to mix your business finances with your personal finances. Open new accounts for your business. These include:

- Business checking account
- PayPal account
- Credit card

Collecting Sales Tax
This is required if:

- Your state of operation collects sales tax.
- Someone in your state places an order.

In most places, a business license is necessary, and you must renew it regularly. Check your local regulations and laws to see what you may need. As a storeowner, you put in a lot of work to offer a great experience to your customers. You enhance your store, write emails, and edit photos just so your customers can be happy. Therefore, shipping can be a challenge. It is like having a stranger handle your brand. Careful planning will make this easier. Here are key steps and decisions that set the foundation for your shipping strategy. You can always change them as you grow. Shipping methods and rates: are you going to offer flat-rate or free shipping? Alternatively, will your customers have to cover the shipping cost? Product weights: how much do your products weigh? Your preferred packaging: having a packaging option in mind will help you estimate the shipping price. Source the packaging: get free packaging from DHL, UPS and USPS. You can also opt for branded packaging. Your pricing strategy will determine your shipping rates. You can offer free shipping and raise the price of the products or pay from your profits. You can also balance both. Another option is to choose flat rate shipping or charge real-time carrier rates.

Calculate Shipping Costs

Shipping rates are often based on the following:

- Destination country
- Origin country
- Package weight
- Package size

Other options like insurance and tracking are involved as well. Consider your profit margins. As you do your calculations, incorporate all costs involved. Packaging is not just about getting the product to the customer. Buyers have higher expectations. You need to compete effectively by going out of your way to impress customers. Offer your buyers an exceptional unboxing experience. The common packaging options include envelopes and boxes. Uline has a wide range of shipping materials for all your needs. Other packaging suppliers include eSupplyStore, Fast-Pack, and ValueMailers. Tracking and shipping insurance offer security. Carriers do not charge much for this service. If you can, buy insurance on big-ticket products to ensure that you are covered when your package gets lost. Some couriers incorporate insurance in their shipping costs. Have this in mind when comparing courier prices. Proper customs documentation is required if your shipping to another country. The forms are available at the shipping retail location or your local post office. Make sure you fill up the forms clearly and honestly— otherwise, your package may get held in Customs. In your shipping policy page, include any additional custom fees that that the customer may be required to pay on delivery. After deciding on the carrier, it is time to set up business accounts. These accounts have tons of benefits for your business. Labelling your packages by hand can be tedious and time consuming. If you are using Shopify, you can pay for their labelling service to save time. A fulfillment warehouse gives you benefits such as short shipping times and cheap shipping rates. They also have disadvantages; but perform your due diligence.

Chapter 1
DropShipping Details

There are many details involved in running a successful dropshipping business. They can be summarized into two key principles: Things may get messy, accept that: sometimes, the involved third-party can complicate things. Adopt a KISS mentality: KISS stands for Keep It Simple, Stupid! Go for the easy-to-implement solutions even though they may not be perfect.

When an Order Is Botched

Suppliers will make mistakes; even the best ones. This is what you do when one messes up. Own the mistake: do not blame anyone. Apologize and promise to fix it. Make it up to the customer: do something to fix the error. You can refund the shipping fee or offer an upgrade. Make your supplier pay: you need to own the mistake but not necessarily pay for it. The supplier may not pay for the freebies, but he or she should pay for other accrued expenses.

Managing Multiple Suppliers and Inventory

One of the biggest challenges for dropshippers is managing the inventory. The practices below will help you have less out-of-stock items. Have multiple suppliers: when the first supplier does not have a certain item, the second one will probably have it. Choose products wisely: sell items that are sold by the two suppliers. You will have two options of fulfillment. Utilize generics: when two suppliers carry different but identical items, make your product description generic and list both model numbers. Check the item availability; be in constant communication with the sales representative to know what is available. Out-of-stock orders: even if you plan perfectly, at one time you will be unable to fulfill an order. Try offering a complimentary upgrade (like the product) instead of just telling the customer that it is out of order.

Order Fulfillment

Route order to the preferred supplier: have a "favorite" supplier and have all orders go to him by default. Route based on location: always route the customer's order to the suppler nearest to them. Route based on availability: this can be a hectic option but there are services such as eCommHub. Route based on price: this is easier in theory than in practice.

Fraud and Security

Credit card numbers: storing the credit card data of your customers is convenient but it is risky. Just avoid it. Fraudulent orders: be cautious and use common sense to avoid this pitfall. Address verification system: the AVS prevents thieves from making successful purchases.

Be alert when you notice the following:

- Different shipping and billing
- Different names
- Strange email address
- Expedited shipping

Understanding Cashbacks

When you get a cashback, act quickly. Present all documents that are required to prove the order was fulfilled. You may lose the case if the billing and shipping addresses are different.

Dealing with Returns

Check your suppliers' return policies before you write your own. Also, consider things that can complicate the process such as restocking fees, defective items, etc.

Shipping Issues

You can use any of these three forms of shipping rates:

- Real-time rates
- Per-type rates
- Flat-rate shipping

Customer Support

An Excel spreadsheet will not be of much help here. Try these options:

- Help Scout
- Zendesk
- Desk
- Kayako

For phone support, try:

- Grasshopper
- RingCentral

Chapter 2
Successful Email Marketing

E ven with the rise of social media, email is still an important part of most people's lives. So, if you are an entrepreneur, one of the best things you can do for your business is build a lucrative email marketing campaign. Many people, however, have no idea how too. Everywhere people look they are met with advertisements, pitches, and all kinds of interruption. Although you might think yours is unique, the reader, most likely, cannot tell the difference. Never forget the space that you are in and always have your best manners. Being in another person's inbox is like being invited over to their house for dinner. If your host requires you to take off your shoes, you do not argue. The same case applies to email marketing, it is their personal space and you must be respectful. Acquiring permission is the first step to having a successful email marketing campaign. You need to have a sizable email list. You might do this by giving freebies, offering product updates, or a newsletter. There is no right or wrong way between the two, provided you express a clear purpose when requesting someone's address. Make people excited to give their addresses instead of just writing, "enter your email for updates". Great email service providers strive to ensure that major ISPs do not block your emails. They have no control of where your emails end up; spam box or inbox. Getting whitelisted ensures proper delivery of your emails. You get whitelisted by having your recipient add you to their address book. Always give instructions on how to do this in every email. Set your expectations. A strong call-to-action and consistent follow-up is the ingredients of a positive campaign. Do not promise to send out one email in a week and then send emails every day—deliver on your promise, whatever it is. Step in your reader's shoes if you plan to pitch often. Your messaging should be consistent with the expectations you set. Always ask yourself what value you are adding. The best newsletters, for most readers, are those that mix updates and messaging properly. When you are sending out a newsletter with images and product updates, try to include a friendly update or personal message. Instead of talking to your list only when you have something to sell, utilize autoresponder and schedule content for consistent delivery. It helps to be in touch and have a relationship with your list. The three most crucial analytics are unsubsribers, click through rate (CTR), and open rate. Open rate tells you whether people read or delete your email upon receipt. A low CTR means your message is not getting through. A high unsubscription rate means you have a lot of work to do. Segmentation is splitting your list into targeted groups. Segmenting your list helps you send targeted emails. Your email list is a very valuable resource and if you run your email marketing campaign right, the ROI will be high. Email is not dead. It is a crucial component of any marketing plan and allows you to reach the audience conveniently when you need to. However, people receive countless emails in their inboxes daily, how do you make sure yours are unique? And where should an email marketing newbie begin? Even if readers have subscribed to your email-marketing program, you still need to outshine the hundreds of emails that flow into their inboxes and make sure yours gets opened. Captivating subject lines are essential to increasing open rates. Do not be in a hurry and skim through this vital process. It is also the first thing that your readers see. For your email goals to be successful, you need to allow fans to subscribe to your emails. Include a subscription form in your website and on your business Facebook page, allowing customers to opt in your email list. Whenever you attend events, collect as many email addresses as you can. Your readers should know what they are signing up for. An ESP (Email Service Provider) will do a great job deploying your email blasts.

Email Service Providers help you create designed emails, view performance records, manage unsubscribe requests, and your address list. An ESP also offers you a collection of prebuilt templates making it possible for you to design emails without having coding skills. Almost half of your subscribers open their email on a mobile device. Consider your email audience while designing or selecting an email template. Most ESPs indicate whether a template is mobile friendly or not. Do not make an email 100% about selling your product. It is a great opportunity to create a relationship with your audience and promote your brand. Balance promotional and informative content for you to have a trusting and loyal subscriber base. Have test accounts with the most popular email clients (Outlook, AOL, Gmail, and Yahoo) to see how your email appears to different readers. Send a copy to each of your "testing addresses" before you send to your audience. Email ending up in spam instead of inbox is a common problem. Subscribe to your newsletter using several email platforms with a testing email or your personal email. After sending an email, check your inbox, and if they land in the spam folder almost every time, you have a problem and you should contact your ESP. What time should you send your email? Should your name be in the subject line? You can only know the answers by experimenting because every subscriber base is different. Know what the law requires of you and adhere to it. For US citizens, there is the CAN-SPAM Act that governs sending out emails. Be consistent to keep the readers engaged and maintain a healthy relationship with them. Anytime you are developing a newsletter, remember that you are crafting it for people who are curious to hear from you. Your newsletter is an awesome opportunity to make your loyal readers have an interest in your new book or business and maintain a relationship with them between publications.

With that knowledge, here is a rundown of what you might want to include:

- Clear publication and book details
- A short account of the writing process or research
- Current events or articles of interest
- Behind the scene photos and/or information
- Important links: social media links, subscribe/unsubscribe link, retailer links and author website links

There isn't a definite rule about the frequency of newsletters but to be more effective, let it be regularly and consistently. Some people prefer to send them out more regularly when the publication date is around the corner because they have much to talk about with the audience. Consult your editorial and marketing teams and ask them to help you figure out the best time to share with your audience news of your book just before its publication. No two publications are the same but the following general milestones are worth considering as content of your newsletter. Send your subscribers a message breaking the news of your book officially. In it; reveal the on-sale date, title, and the book jacket (if available). Share the official book description and anecdotes of your writing process. Have your marketing team provide links for the readers to preorder the book. Note; wait until online retailers have your book information up before you make the announcement. Your editor might help you choose a short excerpt for your readers. The excerpt can be included in the newsletter's body or just have a link that leads back to the full excerpt. You should always accompany the excerpt with retailer links for readers to easily order the book. Remind your subscribers of your book release with a countdown email. This builds up excitement among your audience and reminds them where and how to get the book. Let readers know of any tour or event planned at publication. Reveal the locations and dates and even give links to the platform on which the event will be airing live. Send a newsletter celebrating publication and remind them about buying the book. Even after publications (or between publications) engage your readers regularly. It is not easy to find content to share with subscribers during this period. Hopefully these ideas will help:

- Thoughts on the writing process and research
- Short essays (could be unrelated to your publication)
- The book you are currently reading
- Your social media platforms
- Giveaways/exclusive offers
- Q&As with relevant personalities (like other authors)

The content you share in your newsletter may overlap with what you share on your website, social media, and blog, which is okay. Your newsletter should focus on crucial information or longer-form content. On social media, share content that may not be appropriate for a newsletter. Work hard to grow your subscriber list by making the subscriber button available in every newsletter; having a sign-up form in your website, utilizing social media, and making content more interesting.

Chapter 3
The Fulfillment Process

Supply chain basically refers to the path taken by a product from its conception, to its manufacturing and eventually to the customer's hands. Supplier chain gurus will insist that the supply chain begins at mining of the raw materials—but that is a bit too intense. This chapter will focus on the three key players in the drop shipping supply chain. They include manufacturers, wholesalers, and retailers. Manufacturers: they make the product and barely sell it to the public directly. Instead, they sell, it to retailers and wholesale in bulk. It is cheaper to buy a product from a manufacturer directly, but some manufacturers have purchase requirements in place. The better option is to buy from a wholesaler. Wholesalers: buy items from manufacturers in bulk. They slightly mark them up, and sell to retailers who, in turn, resale to the final consumer. Although some of them have set up purchasing minimums, they are more likely to be lower than those of manufacturers. Retailers: sell items to the public directly. If you fulfill your customers' orders through a dropshipping supplier, then you have a retail business. Drop shipping is not included in the supply chain above. Any of the three players listed can be dropshippers. If a manufacturer ships their products to your customers directly, they are drop shipping. The same way, a retail merchant can dropship. Not every drop shipping company will offer you wholesale pricing. The company will ship goods on your behalf. If you want the best pricing, you will have to look for a legitimate manufacturer or wholesaler and work with them. How exactly are dropshipping orders processed? Take the example of Phone Outlet, a theoretical online store for smartphone accessories. All its products are directly dropshipped from Wholesale Accessories, a wholesaler.

This is the process:

Step 1: Placing the Order

Mr. Foster wants a new smartphone case, so he places an order through Phone Outlet. After the order has been approved, the following happen: An email confirmation is sent to Mr. Foster and Phone Outlet about the new order. When Mr. Foster pays in the checkout process the payment is captured and deposited into the bank account of the online merchant.

Step 2: Phone Outlet Places the Order

This is a very simple step. Phone Outlet forwards the email confirmation to Wholesale Accessories (a sales representative, specifically). Phone Outlet's credit card is on file, so they bill it for the total amount, including shipping.

Step 3: Shipping the Order

When the wholesaler successfully charges the credit card, they box up the item and ship it to the customer directly. The name and address on the return address label is that of Phone Outlet and so is the logo.

Step 4: Alerting the Customer

After Phone Outlet receives the invoice and tracking number, they send the customer the tracking information. This signifies the completion of the entire process.

Chapter 4
Finding and Working with Suppliers

The key point is to be able to tell between retail stores pretending to be wholesale suppliers and legitimate wholesale suppliers. A real supplier gets their products from the manufacturer directly and you will get better pricing with them. How Do You Tell Whether a Drop shipping Wholesaler Is Fake? There are so many scamming "wholesalers". The legitimate ones usually have poor marketing strategy and are hard to find. The middlemen, therefore, will frequently appear in your searches. This is how you tell whether a supplier is legitimate. They ask for ongoing fees: true wholesalers do not impose a monthly fee on their customers for doing business with them. Note that there is a difference between a supplier directory and a supplier. The former will charge a fee, but it is not because they are illegitimate. Selling to the public: a supplier that sells products to the public at supposedly wholesale prices is simply a retailer selling at inflated prices. There are, however, legitimate drop shipping fees such as: Per-order fees: the fee is about $2-$5. It is a per-order dropshipping fee charged by most dropshippers. Minimum order size: several wholesalers have set a minimum size of order. You cannot order lower than the set amount for your first order.

Finding Wholesale Suppliers

Now that you know how to tell a fraud from a real supplier, the next step is to search for wholesalers. The list of strategies below is in order of effectiveness.

Contact the Manufacturer

If you have already decided on a product, contact the manufacturer and request a list of their wholesale distributors. Next, contact the wholesalers on the list and ask whether they dropship and how you should go about the process of creating an account.

Use Orbelo

In several clicks, you can import goods into your Shopify store. You get the products from the supplier directly and ship to your customers.

Search Using Google

Although this one seems obvious, you need to have a few rules in mind:

- Perform an extensive search.
- Avoid judging by the website.
- Make good use of modifiers.

Order from the Competition

This is how you achieve it: look for a dropshipping competitor and order from them. Once the package arrives, check the return address and Google it to know the original shipper.

Attend a Trade Show

You will meet key wholesalers and manufacturers in a specific niche.

Directories

Many of these directories are managed by for-profit organizations and you may, therefore, must pay a fee.

Some good directories include:

- Worldwide Brands
- SaleHoo
- Doba
- Wholesale Central

Before You Talk to a Supplier

Once you have a list of reputable suppliers, it is time to take the next step and contact them. Before you do, however, you need to make sure everything is in order. Be legal. legitimate wholesalers will want to work with legal businesses. Be careful how you appear. Do not shy away from calling the supplier of your choice. Sourcing products can be a huge pain for entrepreneurs. In this chapter, a supplier is anyone who can provide inventory and products. It may be a distributor, wholesaler or manufacturer. First, understand what kind of supplier you want. When you figure this out, you will know what to type in when searching. These are the most common options:

- Dropshipper
- Supplier
- Manufacturer

Overseas Vs Domestic Suppliers

If you want to wholesale or manufacture, you must decide whether you will source from abroad or domestically. Typically, overseas suppliers are in Taiwan, India, China and other Asian countries. They are popular because they offer cheap options. However, cost is not the only factor worth considering when making this decision. There are advantages and disadvantages of sourcing both domestically and from abroad. The internet is a great to begin your search. However, if you are looking for specific places, try the following. Directories: free supplier directories can be found online, and they tend to be very helpful. You will find thousands of profiles for suppliers, wholesalers and manufacturers. The best domestic directories include Kompass, MFG, Maker's Row and ThomasNet. The best overseas directories include Sourcify, IndiaMart, AliExpress, Alibaba, and Oberlo. Google: supplier websites are not the most attractive. You may have to go to the second page of the Google search results to find them. Local library: you would be surprised how useful local libraries can be. Referrals: feel free to ask your professional networks for recommendations. If you can find successful people in your niche, the better. Another useful way is searching for the NAICS (North American Industry Classification System) code of your products. Suppliers and manufacturers sometimes list their products using the NAICS code. This makes it easier to find the supplier for your specific products. The NAICS directory is easily accessible online or at your local library. Once you have a list of several possibilities, research further to check their credibility. The Better Business Bureau (BBB) will show you if any complaints have been filed against them. Facebook and Google reviews will also tell you a lot. Approaching your supplier is the next step. The price they will charge is probably the biggest issue in your mind. However, make sure you plan your questions and words beforehand.

In your email, consider these important factors:

- Your MOQ (minimum order quantity)
- Your sample pricing
- Your production pricing
- Your turnaround times
- Your payment terms

If you are doing this for the first time, you will soon hear about MOQs. Manufacturers may require you to buy thousands or, at least, hundreds of units as your first order. This depends on the manufacturer and the product. When you do not have much money, MOQs can be difficult. Fortunately, they are negotiable in most cases. Before you get into negotiations, understand the position of the supplier first then offer a lower MOQ.

Chapter 5
Picking Products to Dropship

Picking a niche is a huge hurdle for people that are new to dropshipping. This is a crucial decision with long-term consequences. Choosing a product based on your passion or personal interest is a big mistake; that is, if your aim is to make a profit. This is what you must do for your ecommerce business to be successful: Create your own product: you will be the only source of that product and can control distribution. You will barely have competition which lets you charge a great price. Be able to access exclusive distribution or pricing: if you cannot manufacture your own product, talk to a manufacturer and see if you can get exclusive pricing. Offer competitive pricing: when you are selling at the lowest price, you will attract customers from other businesses. The problem with this strategy is that it is a recipe for failure. Pricing wars will strip you of profits. Add value: you can set your business apart by offering important information in relation to your product. Add value in ecommerce: look for a niche that makes it easy to add value along with educational content. High-quality images: the images should give customers a good idea of what they are getting. Multiple components: if a product needs any components, you will have a great opportunity of adding value. Confusing and/or customizable: products that are both customizable and confusing are perfect as far as adding value via content is concerned. Require installation or technical setup: this allows you to offer expert guidance.

How to Add Value to Confusing and Technical Niches

- Make comprehensive guides for buyers.

- Write detailed listings and product descriptions.
- Create setup and installation guides.
- Make in-depth videos on how the product works.
- Come up with an easy-to-follow system.

Picking the Best Customers
Here are some of the clients that will benefit your business.
Hobbyists: people can spend ridiculous amounts because of their hobbies.
Businesses: they place huge orders in most cases.
Repeat buyers: they ensure recurring revenue.
Other Factors to Consider When Choosing Products

- Perfect price
- MAP pricing
- Marketing potential
- Lots of accessories
- Low turnover
- Hard to get locally
- The smaller the better

Measuring Demand
No matter how good your product is, you will not make profit if no one wants it. Here are online tools that help you measure a product's demand. Google Keyword Tool: this shows the number of people searching for the product. Google Trends: this one offers more details than the Google Keyword Tool.
Measuring Competition
These metrics help you quickly evaluate the strength of competition. Number of linking domains: if a site has multiple links on it, then it is powerful. Authority of competing websites: the number of links is not the only thing that matters, the quality of these links is considered as well. Qualitative metrics: these include site quality, site

reputation, etc. Search results: use "incognito" mode on Chrome or force nation-specific results for unbiased search results. In a studied case, the business is built around making coconut hair oil. The evaluation process involves asking yourself questions. Perfect answers are not exactly necessary; you can make educated guesses. These criteria focus on external factors such as trending trajectory, target customer, and market size, among others. It is not easy to perfectly gauge the demand or marketer size, but you should have an idea before investing resources. Make use of services such as Google Keyword Planner Tool or Buzzsumo. In Canada and the USA alone, there were more than 73,000 searches for "coconut oil for hair" and related keywords per month. This means that there are interested. Who are you competing against? Know you competitors to avoid surprises in future. In the coconut oil for hair market, there are three main competition areas; commercial coconut products for hair, DIY recipes for coconut oil, and pure coconut oil. Is it a growing market, a trend or just a fad? You need to know the direction of the market. The search for coconut oil, according to Google Trends, has been growing over the last years. Can your target customers buy it locally? If they can already buy the product locally, they may not be interested in looking for it online. Who are you targeting? Use Twitter to see who is searching for your product. What is your selling price? Check other similar products from similar companies to see the average price. With that price, what will be your profit margin? What is your markup? The markup will be your profit and cover your overhead. Consider the cost of raw materials and production. Compared to the selling price, can you enjoy a healthy markup? How many SKU's will you stock? SKU's are styles and types of products. The more you stock, the more hectic the business will be. Will you offer a subscription? Being able to offer a subscription increases lifetime customer value. A subscription would not work with coconut oil because people are likely to use it as needed. What is the weight and size of your product? Heavy products are expensive to ship and may turn away customers. Is your product durable? The more durable the product, the better. You will pay less for shipping. Will you have to deal with seasonality swings? Seasonality wings will affect your cash flow. Coconut oil is not quite affected by seasonality swings. Does your product solve a pain or serve a passion? Product that solve a pain are more marketable. Coconut oil, for instance, solves the pain of dry hair. Is your product disposable or consumable? Disposable or consumable products are likely to win you repeat customers. Is the product perishable? Perishable products are a recipe for disaster if you do not make sales. Is your product regulated or limited? Knowing this will help you plan and be prepared.

Chapter 6
Evaluating Sales Channels

Now that you have legally established your business, picked out a product and secured suppliers, you need to do sell, sell, sell. There are several available sales options. Possibly, you are only going to select one or maybe a combination. eBay is the largest online auction site in the world, for physical goods.

Benefits of Selling on eBay

Easy to start: As soon as you create your account you can add the listings and start selling. A large audience: eBay is visited by so many people daily. Your listings will be visible to millions of potential buyers. Less marketing: eBay is an enormous platform and you automatically get a large audience.

The Downsides

Listing fees: eBay fees are a huge disadvantage. The success fee is the most notable one as it can be 10% or higher. The margins in the dropshipping market are already thin and this may greatly slice your profits. Constant Re-Listing and Monitoring: since this is an auction marketplace, you must monitor and re-list your products on a regularly. There are automation tools that can help with this process, but it is still more hectic than listing a static item on your website. Your sales platform is not customizable: you must list your products using the eBay templates. Connection with customers: sometimes, you will have repeat customers on eBay but often, this will not be the case. Your communication with customers is limited. You are not creating an asset: your eBay store is not a lasting brand. It does not have value and you cannot sell it in future.

Dropshipping on Amazon

Amazon mainly sells through third-party merchants.

Benefits of Selling on Amazon

The benefits you will reap from selling Amazon are quite like those of eBay: the starting process is easy; you can access a large audience and marketing will not be a big issue for you. Amazon also has fulfillment warehouses which are a huge advantage.

Disadvantages of Selling on Amazon

Listing fees: much like eBay, commission fees can be high.

Exposure of sales data: Amazon has full access to your sales data and they sometimes use it to their advantage. Connection with customers: they are no different from eBay. No customization: again, Amazon is just like eBay in this area and you will be limited.

Your Own Online Store

This is the most attractive dropshipping channel.

Benefits of Your Own Store

More control: you can customize the shopping environment to suit your products.

Easy design: platforms such as Shopify make it easy for you. Mobile ready: Amazon and eBay may be a pain when you are selling via mobile. No third-party fees: your profit margins will improve significantly. A real business: your own shop will be like a real shop with repeat customers and a unique experience. You can also sell it.

The Downsides

Less free traffic: you will have to work for traffic through SEO, paid advertising, and marketing.

Chapter 7
Social Media Marketing Strategy

People already spend time on social platforms and through social media marketing, you can build an engaged audience. This way, you will have several sources of traffic and, consequently, growth in your business. Social media marketing can also drain you and produce no positive results at all. The difference between the above two scenarios is a social media marketing strategy. This comprehensive guide will show you how to do it like a pro.

Creating a Social Media Strategy

Before anything, understand what you are looking for. What do you hope to achieve from social media marketing? Your business can amass the following benefits, brand awareness, increased sales and traffic, engaged audience, support for customers, and much more.

Defining a Social Media Marketing Strategy

Here are five key pillars to adhere to when coming up with a social media strategy:

Goals: note what you aim to achieve and how you will measure your achievements. Target audience: know and research your ideal customer. Content mix: build social media programming anchored on recurring content archetypes. Channels: select the suitable social networks for your purpose.

Process: have in place the tools and infrastructure to follow your strategy.

Setting Goals

Your goals should be reflected in your posts so define them in advance. Check out some of these great goals that you can consider:

- Driving brand awareness
- Acquiring leads
- Getting sales
- Driving online traffic
- Networking
- Getting a loyal following
- Establishing social proof
- Offering customer service

Identifying the Target Audience

Research your target audience. Look for any observable patterns. Check out the people that are most likely to buy from your business. This step is easier if you are running a niche business. After your digging, build your "buyer persona" or ideal customer. Fill out their traits.

- Location
- Age
- Relationship status
- Income level
- Gender
- Interests
- Career/industry
- Favorite apps/sites
- Motivation to buy
- Buying concerns
- Other info

Creating Content for Social Media

What recurring post types and formats will you rely on? To do this efficiently, answer the following question: "Other than your product, can you offer value consistently to your audience?"

Try incorporating the following in your content mix:

- News
- Inspiration
- Education
- Promotional posts
- Giveaways and contests
- Influencer/customer features
- Community events
- Q&A
- Behind-the-scenes

Allow Customers to Contribute

Depending on what products you sell, you can encourage your customers to submit before and after pictures using your branded hashtag. You can then share the photos on your shoppable Instagram page.

Shots of the Product in Use

This is an amazing way to drive sales.

Humor Relating to Your Audience

Funny posts can make your audience engage more. Leverage funny videos and memes.

Prioritize Channels for Your Strategy

You have more than one option as far as social media channels are concerned. Make sure you:

- Choose only as many channels as you can maintain.
- Utilize the strengths of each one.

Executing Your Plan

Collect ideas and plan your content. Next schedule your content. There are great tools for this like:

- Later
- Hootsuite

- Buffer

Chapter 8
Driving Sales with Content Marketing

Regardless of what you are selling, content marketing will make a difference in your business. When you share valuable content for free, you build your brand, offer information to customers, create trust, and rank on search engines. Even better, you attract prospects through content marketing and convert them into customers. These customers may then become repeat buyers. How can you, and other ecommerce companies, create content that will attract followers and fans? This is how top online stores can win with their content. How-to videos easily hook people and make them glued to your content. They are even more useful to niche websites. Take Luxy Hair, for instance. They specialize in clip-in hair extensions which give you fuller hair. They have set up a YouTube channel that is as awesome as the product itself. Through their videos, customers learn how to store the extensions, select the perfect shade, what to do when their hair is short, and step-by-step tutorials. Additionally, they have videos that are not remotely related to hair extensions. They show women how to make a messy bun, soft ponytail, and how to blow-dry their own hair.

Be like Luxy Hair:

- Explain your product with how-to videos
- Make unrelated how-tos
- Leverage the power of teaching

Answer Your FAQs Creatively

FAQ pages are common among ecommerce sites. They answer common questions asked by customers and enhance customer support.

Zirtual have an "Examples" page. It clearly outlines their services (virtual assistance). Although they are not exactly an ecommerce site, they show that content does not have to be boring. REI is an ecommerce site that sells outdoor sporting gear. They answer real questions asked by their customers using how-to videos.

Be like REI and Zirtual:

- Answer your customers' questions creatively.
- Use FAQs to get content ideas

Photo-Heavy Content

The purpose of an ecommerce site is to make sales. The better images you have of the product, the higher your chances of selling. Businesses like VivaLaJewels post their products on Instagram and wow their followers. One Kings Lane have magazine-quality photos on their site, along with informational content.

Be like One Kings Lane:

- Splash beautiful images of the product on your site.
- Fill your blog with products.

Become a Media Outlet for Yourself

If you want to stand out in your niche, becoming a publisher is a good idea. Create a space where your followers can get information. This separates you from companies that are just selling. This media outlet will make people trust you, view you as an authority, and you will enjoy a lot of traffic.

Be like Kempt and Urban Daddy:

- Have different media outlets.
- Become a publisher.

Be in the Know

Birchbox is a beauty ecommerce site. In addition to offering beauty products, they engage in tough conversations with their customers. They talk about self-image issues and other issues surrounding women, beauty, and society.

Be like Birchbox:

- Take a stand on societal issues.
- Embrace controversy.

Chapter 9

Etsy Shop

E tsy is an online retail community just like eBay only that it focuses on vintage or handcrafted commodities. Most of the goods sold there are in the jewelry, arts, crafts, housewares, artisan candies, baked goods, or paper-goods categories. For an item to qualify as vintage it must be at least 20 years old and can be anything from photos, costumes, housewares, jewelry, and clothing. Etsy provides a great avenue for you to sell your homemade goods—but that's not all. You can find a limitless number of items on Etsy that will help your home business. For instance, if you use The Happy Planner, Filofax, or Erin Condren to schedule and organize your life or business, there are downloadable stickers and inserts that you can buy and use in your planner. If you need promotional items that have your logo on them; there are a good number of Etsy sellers that can make custom swag for you. They will not only make coffee cups and pens, but also cosmetics, jewelry, bookmarks, and pretty much everything with your logo and name on them. For a very long time, most artisans and craftsman sold their commodities at open markets, fairs, and on consignment. Although the Internet widened their market, most craftsmen did not want to go through the trouble of creating their own e-commerce platform, website, or credit card processor just to sell goods online. Sure, eBay and maybe other e-commerce DIY sites might have helped with the situation, but Etsy offered a platform designed specifically for craftsman. Etsy makes it easy for each seller to create an online "shop" with total e-commerce capabilities with the easy-to-use set-up wizard. It is a simple, affordable, fast, and convenient way of reaching customers. Creating an Etsy storefront will cost you $0.20 for every item listed. For instance, if you sell handmade baskets, and you list four of them (of the same kind), the cost will be 4 x $0.20 = $0.80. In addition, you will be charged a 3.5 % transaction fee. If you decide to use the "Direct Checkout" feature, you will be charged a 3% fee for each transaction. If you compare the total cost of creating a website that has a shopping cart and acquiring a merchant account (which also involves processing fees), Etsy is way cheaper. Decide what item you want to sell. If you deal in crafts, you might already have an idea of what you want to sell. You can sell multiple products. However, it is advisable to start with one type as you learn. Set up an Etsy account. The first step is coming up with a username. Make sure it represents your product and at the same time remains open in case you decide to expand your product line. Set up and stock your shop. When adding your products, remember that great photos and product descriptions are important. Price your items wisely too. Provide excellent customer service. You want the buyers to leave nice reviews. When a product is in demand, keep the supply steady to build a lucrative home-crafting business. Posting a standalone video on YouTube can help promote your business. Unlike Snapchat videos and Instagram stories that expire after a short time, evergreen videos on YouTube are there to stay and can be used as a reference and even be distributed on any platform. You may include a FAQ video link on the about page of your Etsy shop or have a short DIY and share it on all social networks. Creating videos featuring your production process, your products, and help customers connect with you on a deeper level, bridging the gap that exists between small craft retail and the cold nature of online retail. YouTube videos also widen your market hence more customers. The following suggestions will help you make an amazing first video. If you are just starting your video channel, a quick introduction gives the viewers context. In a minute or two, tell them who you are, where you are based, what you sell, and the story of how your business came to be.

Do not be afraid to share the video on all your social networks, encouraging your followers to subscribe to the channel. Take a step further and have this introduction video link in your press pitch emails. Consumers are more compelled to buy a handmade product more when they learn and respect the creative process. Capture the parts that make up your product in various stages. For instance, capture the entire knitting process of a hat from beginning to end. When you list a new product in your shop, consider posting a release video to generate a buzz and attract your customers' attention. Share relevant details about your product to spice things up a bit, share the story of what inspired its production or what is so special about it. Any online seller who has been in the business long enough knows that very few shoppers read written FAQs and policies. Use the video as an opportunity to address a few common questions. Use interesting visuals and sound effects to keep them engaged. A video of your product being used in context will also show the function of the item clearly and allow customers to envision themselves using it. Do enough research on your target market to find out how buyers are likely to use the product. This will help you present your product perfectly and answer relevant questions. Original instructional videos will attract viewers and encourage social sharing. Think of content that complements your products and brand in general; for example, a "quick tips" series on maybe styling your pieces. Short "How To" is also well loved by viewers. Storyboarding is the primary element in shooting a tutorial video. It does not have to be complex; a simple listing of what will happen in the video is enough. The shorter the video; the better, speed up or trim long, boring steps. The video should be clear. Zoom in where necessary so viewers can properly see the finer details. Experiment a little with various styles and be keen on statistics to see how the videos are doing. Be true to yourself and your business in order to create compelling content. All new sellers are faced with the question of how they can increase views and purchases on their Etsy shop. There is no secret shortcut, but the keys below will do the job. Sell something that you love; you should love and believe in whatever you are selling. As a new seller, you probably have other commitments. If you sell what you love you will be motivated. Get inspired; what would you love to have but can't find it out there? Read lots of blogs and magazines to see what people are buying and wearing then check on Etsy. The aim is not to copy another seller but to inspire ideas. Do research; what is that great product that very few people (or none) are selling on Etsy? Bringing something different to the market will make you stand out. Get found; Usually, buyers stumble on your shop from a product listing through search. It could also be featured elsewhere. Having more items increases your chances of being found. How many items? What you sell is the determinant here. If your items are time-intensive and expensive then you will most likely stock fewer items. Look at shops that are successfully selling what you are selling. The number of items they have in stock should give you a rough idea. Start with what you have; even if you have only one item, go on and list it. Do not sit around waiting to build an inventory. Creating more merchandise and adding more products should be an ongoing goal, not a requirement for getting started. Looks are everything; captivating photos will attract shoppers from search results and even enable your product to be featured on Etsy and all over the Internet. Take the click ability test; Try searching for your product and evaluate the other products on the page. Which photo makes you want to click on it? Is it yours? If not, learn something from those that make you want to click on them. Bring your product to life; since a shopper can neither see nor touch your item, let your photos communicate all the details to them. Search suggestions; try to figure out what shoppers are searching for. Type your item into the search box with vintage, supplies, or handmade selected. The words and phrases that appear are customers' popular searches. Improve your chances; utilize all of your tags by entering popular phrases and keywords likely to be used by buyers. Let your titles contain a lot of accurate and descriptive terms. Bonus key, ship internationally, Sell all over the world; selling globally increases your chances of selling. Let more people find you. If you want to appear in searches by shoppers from other countries, make sure your product ships to their country (include the destination "Everywhere Else"). Do not let international shipping intimidate you. It is not difficult. On your shipping carrier's website, you will get the average rates for shipping "Everywhere Else". In conclusion, get rid of policies that are not working. Ever since Apple launched iPhone eight years ago, the world has seen a mobile revolution that has completely changed how humans interact with their environment. Mobile apps continue to become a huge part of day-to-day life. Mobile devices contribute to more than half of traffic to Etsy and shop owners are keenly watching. Tammy King from OurVintageBungalow realized that this is a trending source of traffic that she cannot overlook. She started visiting her shop using her phone as a buyer in order to see what they saw. Just as you take your shop image and branding seriously, you should do the same about your mobile presence. Going by mobile shop trends, chances are that shoppers come across your shop as they browse the Etsy app. The tips below, therefore, will help you make a great impression on shoppers. Shopping on a mobile device mostly involves discovering new products and shops as you browse. A shopper starts out the shopping journey on one device but ends it on another, according to the Group product Manager for Mobile at Etsy, Arpan Podduturi. It is likely that a shopper browses the app as they commute and then comes back later when they have decided to make a purchase. On Etsy, they may favorite a shop or save it for a later time. Enticing photos and a captivating about page will draw their attention. Looking at her shop in the Etsy app, owner of MenemshaJewelry, Menemsha Abeyasekera, knew that something needed to be done about the photos. Your first photo on every listing should communicate to a potential customer what the item is. Among the many things that a buyer is likely to see first is the photo; make it a good one. It should be of high impact and quality. The listing page space on a smaller device, like a phone, is way smaller than on a desktop display; use the small space wisely. Roy Stanfield who is a Senior Product Designer at Etsy gives insight on a method that he uses with his team to make design decisions. Consider the most important details of your product and list them. Your title should be brief and every crucial detail about your item should be at the top. That is the first thing a buyer will see. Mobile visits are increasing, and they will continue to be, according to market trends. Mobile should be part of your workflow now, just as it is Tammy's. She advises that part of your everyday job should be making your shop viewable on the Etsy shop. Checking your mobile storefront regularly will help you make necessary changes. It, therefore, goes without saying that you must have the Etsy app on your phone. Shop Stats shows you how many of your views are from a mobile device. Monitoring and comparing trends let you know whether your listings are drawing mobile shoppers. Check the stats after tweaking titles or images to see if there are changes. Experimenting, as always, will help you know what works and won't for your shop. Most Etsy sellers strive to be found in search by online shoppers. This is a problem that can be easily fixed with time and a little know-how. During the process, think like a buyer. Step 1: Include Attributes In Your Listing; every relevant attribute should be included in the listing. Choose the category that best suits your product in each listing. Depending on the selected category, you can add more attributes to the products like size, color, and whether it can make a great gift. Step 2: Brainstorm Keywords and Phrases; always start with keywords and phrases that the buyer is likely to type in while searching. All your tags, titles, and description should answer each of those questions. Etsy search bar could help you track what shoppers are searching. Type in your item in the search bar; the words that will show up in the drop-down are the words popularly searched by customers. Include the relevant ones in your listing. Try the same with any synonyms you can think of and good keywords that you can find in your listing's description. Do not repeat an attribute that is already on your listing in your 13 tags. Step 3: Apply Search Terms To Your Listings; work your list of keywords and phrases into your product listing. Create Powerful titles; your titles should be buyer-friendly, enticing and have meaningful terms that shoppers are likely to enter while searching. The most important search terms should be at the beginning of your listing. Just because you have your main category included in the title (like vintage, supplies) does not automatically increase your relevance in search for the said items. Nevertheless, it communicates to the shopper. Experiment with words in your title to see which one has a positive effect on your conversion rate. Maximize your tags; use your keywords and phrases in all the available tags. Diversity matters; similar items should not be named the same. Diversify to target many kinds of shoppers. Your most important terms should be in both your tags and titles. Check your statistics to track your results. The information will help you improve your tags, titles, and description. A lot of hits with no sales mean you are probably optimizing for the wrong keywords. If the search terms are yielding results, do not make major changes abruptly. According to Etsy search algorithm, when a shopper favorites, clicks, or purchases a product after coming across it on search, the listing's quality score improves. Encouraging shopper interaction will improve your listing quality. Clear product photographs make a shopper want to click for a closer look. Always double-check to see that your shipping profile is complete to accurately represent your processing times. Also, tell your story in the about section and shop policies. Look for people to help with search terms and improve your ranking.

Chapter 10

Selling on eBay

G o to your preferred search engine and search eBay. Every country has an eBay site tailored to suit it. When searching, go specifically to your country's site. The U.S eBay site is www.ebay.com. Visit the seller information pages. That is where you will find their selling policies, thoroughly discussed. Play around with the search features on eBay. Check out some of the listings. Just seeing other sellers' listings and understanding the search function will help when you decide to make your listings. Go to the "Sort" menu and change the options to see how the search results will change. Take note of the listings that come up at the top and those that seem to get multiple bids. Usually, eBay gives you a name. However, if you pick an attractive name for yourself, your chances of selling may increase. Your name should not be offensive in any way and it should not devalue what you are selling. According to eBay username policies:

- eBay usernames should not have less than two characters. Symbols cannot be part of a username; this includes the hyphen, apostrophe and the 'at' sign.
- The username can neither be an email address or the name of a website. You cannot have the word "eBay" anywhere in your username. It should also not begin with "e" followed by numbers. This policy is to prevent users from posing as eBay employees and to stop sellers from redirecting buyers to less reputable websites.
- Unless you own a trademarked name, you cannot use it as

your username on eBay.

- Avoid unprofessional names because they are likely to repel potential buyers. eBay can also block a name if it is obscene or hateful.
- There are so many sellers on eBay, so it is possible that your desired name is taken. Check to confirm this and think of an alternative name.
- It is possible to change the User ID (only once every 30 days). Avoid changing it too many times, though, lest you lose your repeat customers.

a. Create an Account

On eBay's main page, there is a "sign in" link somewhere at the top. Enter your name and email address then decide on a password. After this step, you will be prompted to select a username.

- eBay will send you an email for you to confirm your account.
- If you already have an existing business, you can open a business account. Go to the sign-up page and look for the "Start a Business Account" link. Fill in the required information.

a. Set Up a Payment Method

The payment methods accepted on eBay vary depending on the country. If you are in the U.S, you should either have a PayPal account or a merchant credit card account. Either use the links on the eBay site to open a PayPal account or go to www.PayPal.com.

- Check out eBay's payment policies to see what methods are allowed in your country.

a. Buy Several Small Items to Build Your Reputation

To ensure safety on the platform, eBay encourages sellers and buyers to leave feedback. Buyers always check out a seller's feedback ratings. Buying some items will quickly give you positive ratings.

- Buy some things that you need or want and pay quickly for positive feedback. You can always resell the items if you do not need them.
- If you have no feedback, potential buyers will be hesitant to buy from you.

a. Complete Your Profile Page

If you are looking to sell small items, you may not need an elaborate profile. But a picture and a little information about yourself will prove your legitimacy to potential buyers.

- If you are selling expensive items, you will have to say more about yourself, more so if you are new.
- Potential sellers read the information to try and know you better. Display your credentials.

1. Choose What to Sell

a. Sell What You Are Knowledgeable About

eBay is a great platform to show off what you have. Specialize in things that you know and enjoy.

a. Know What Is Not Allowed

Obviously, you cannot sell hazardous and illegal items such as live animals, drugs, illicit services and human body parts. There other items that are allowed but restricted. For instance, those that fall under the "adults only" category. Before you start selling, check the banned and restricted items policies. Failure to comply may see your account permanently banned or suspended.

a. Start Small or Just Sell What You Already Have

There are selling limits imposed on new sellers such as only five items in a month. If you have not decided what exactly to sell, you will be taking a big risk if you create an inventory without selling a few items first. List a few things and see what gets the attention of customers and the involved logistics.

- A wise thing to do is selling things around your home that you no longer use.
- Play around first before building an inventory.

a. Know Where and How to Source Your Items

Sourcing items for sale takes effort and time. Before you begin, decide on a sourcing method that you are comfortable with.

- You can even find great bargains on eBay. Maybe look for badly presented and underpriced items or those with misspelled titles.
- Garage sales and thrift stores can also be useful.
- Other places to find great bargains include warehouse, outlet and discount stores. These ones are better because they might have a return policy.

a. Consider the Time It Will Take You to List Each Item

Listing items is not that easy. You need to write descriptions, take pictures and know how every item will be shipped. It is an easier process, though, if you sell similar items.

- Buy items in bulk, if you can, or try to look for items that are similar.
- Find products that are easy to photograph, ship and describe.
- Find products that can be shipped in the same way.

a. Consider Storage and Shipping Logistics

It may be a little difficult to earn profit from heavy and bulky items. They take up so much space and shipping them could be expensive.

- When buyers want to buy an item, they check the total cost and that includes shipping. Consider those when setting the price of your item.
- Do not take the issue of space lightly. Your stock may take up a lot of space and this might be a problem if you are selling from home. Consider setting a separate room for your business.

a. How Quickly Can You Move Your Inventory? How Long Can You Wait?

Trends are always changing and sometimes they change too quickly. If you are not careful, you might end up with stale stock. In other cases, the interested buyer or collector may take some time to turn up.

a. Know What Is Trending

A lot of people search and bid for popular items. Veteran sellers are usually led by their intuition and know what is hot. The good news is that eBay has a way to help you know what is popular.

- There is a hot items' page on eBay, check it out. Fashion accessories, gold, jewelry, brand name clothing, football shirts and electronics are very common here.
- Check out completed listings. This will let you know how much a certain item sells, how much it sells for and when it is sold the most.
- There are products made specifically for sellers to conduct their research. You will, however, must pay for them.
- Understand that popular items will have so many sellers. The competition for buyers will be high.

1. Listings That Sell

a. Research Your Target Market

Go to eBay and search for items like what you are planning to sell. Check the completed and current listings.

- Put yourself in the shoes of a potential buyer and take note of the photos and information that you will find useful.
- Take note of what makes the seller appear trustworthy and incorporate it in your listings.

a. Sign in and Go to "Sell"

a. Create a Title for Your Listings

- Your title is the line that gets your item noticed. In addition to attracting potential buyers who are searching for items on eBay, your title lets them decide whether your listing is worth looking at.

- All relevant words should be included in the title and make sure they are correctly spelled. If the information in the title is too little, fewer people will notice your listing. You may end up selling your items at a very low price or even not selling at all.
- Maintain relevance. Words such as "excellent" and "cool" should not appear in the title. Remember that the space you have is limited so only enter the words that people are likely to search for.
- If the space allows include alternative phrasings and spellings.

a. Take Quality Photos of Your Items

Clear photos attract buyers. Your listing should have at least one photo—the more the photos, the more confident customers will feel.

- Make use of good lighting. Natural light is always better than your camera's flash.
- Edit the photos and enhance any features that may require to be clearer.
- Take many photographs from all angles. You can put up to 12 photos (for free) per listing.
- If an item has any defects, make sure they show in the photo.
- Get rid of dirt and clutter in the background before taking a photo. Neutral backgrounds are the best.
- Do not use photos from other sellers or other sites on the internet. This is fraudulent and dishonest. Moreover, you could get sued for copyright infringement.

a. Write a Description for Your Product

The description should have all the information that is relevant to what you are selling such as compatibility with other items, manufacturer, measurements, condition, etc.

- Be careful not to add too much unnecessary information. A lot of information allows for search engines to find you easily, but a potential buyer can also get bored quickly.
- Important information should be somewhere at the beginning of your listing.
- If you decide to design a listing, keep it simple. Avoid clutter and elements that may make your listing display poorly on mobile devices.
- The text font should be of moderate size and easy to read. Do not use clashing colors and too much animation.
- If your item has any defects, be clear about it. If it has a significant problem, avoid selling it all. You will ruin your reputation.

a. Select a Selling Format

Here, you choose the one that best suits your item and one that you find convenient.

- Online auctions: the auctions last for 1-10 days. They are great because they increase your chances of selling at a high price. They also encourage healthy competition among buyers. This format will suit you if your items are highly sought after.
- Buy-It-Now items: with this format, the item is shipped immediately the buyer buys it.

a. Consider Your Buying Price, eBay Fees, your time, and shipping costs when setting a price

- For auction items, you can change the price before someone places the first bid while for fixed price items you can change it any time.
- When the starting bid is low, more buyers will be attracted to your item which is a good thing. If few people are interested in it, you may end up selling at a very low price.
- You can set a "reserve" price. eBay will charge you extra, though, and buyers do not like this.
- Avoid overcharging for handling and shipping. Nowadays, many sellers offer free shipping and eBay will boost the visibility of your item if you do. Increase the Buy-It-Now price or opening bid and offer your buyers free shipping.
- Take the invoices from eBay seriously and pay on time. Consider the fees business expenses.

a.   Choose When Your Auction Will Start and End

The duration of an auction will determine the price that you sell your item for. If you need to sell at a higher price, schedule the end of your auction at a peak buying time.

- Weekends are a great time to end an auction because then, the traffic is high.
- For seasonal items, consider the time of the year when they are in high demand.
- eBay has planned promotions for some categories. Be sure to check them out.

a.   Maintain a Friendly Tone

Some sellers tend to intimidate potential buyers. Imagine buying from a store as the seller watches your every move like a hawk.

Approach your customers in good faith, not as potential wrongdoers or thieves.

- While writing your policies, make them shorter than your item description.
- It is wise to offer a return policy. You will qualify for eBay discounts and buyers will want to buy even more. Besides, it is very unlikely that a buyer will return an item.
- During an auction, answer your buyers' questions. Be patient, friendly, clear and professional. Also respond promptly.

a. Before You Save, Double-Check Everything

At the "Overview" page, crosscheck everything and then click "Submit". eBay will send you an email telling you that your product is now on eBay.

- Check that you have spelled words correctly. Your listing will be easier to read if you use proper punctuation and capitalization.
- If there are any mistakes, fix them.

1. Completing the Transaction

a. Watch the Auction

Watching the auction will give you an idea. You will know what is working and what is not, then see what to adjust so the listing can be appealing to potential buyers.

- If necessary, end the auction. However, do not make a habit of it. Only use it if you really must (when the item is broken, stolen, or lost).

- Set a low reserve price. If you are not receiving any bids, consider lowering the reserve price.
- You can block buyers if you do not ship to their country, they have unpaid item strikes (two or more), or they do not have a PayPal account.

a. Be Ready to Ship as Soon as the Item Has Been Paid For

a. Package the Item Securely and Neatly

You do not want fragile items to get broken. An excellently packaged product is also a good impression and a buyer may feel confident buying again from you.

a. If a Customer Pays Fast, Leave a Positive Feedback

Take the opportunity to encourage the customer to come back.

1. Promote Your Listings

a. Join eBay Groups If You Sell Handmade Goods or Original Art

These groups consist of artists/crafters who may be collectors or buyers. Engage with hobbyists and be friendly. Avoid flame wars. If you see something you like, compliment.

a. Make Use of Social Networking

Make a blog about your listings. If you have Facebook and Twitter accounts, share them there.

a. When Setting the Minimum Bid or Total Price, Factor in the Shipping Price

Free or cheap shipping will attract buyers and increase their chances of buying.

a. Sell Cheap Items to Build Your Reputation

When two sellers are selling similar or almost similar products, buyers will go for the one with a higher rating.

a. Once You Have Established Your Business, Consider Opening an eBay Shop or Store

You will have your own URL that people can search via search engines. You will be able to sell different categories of items.

1. Tips from Seasoned Sellers

a. Only Sell What You Can Afford to Lose

- Take photos of your products as though there is no description and describe them as though there are no photos.
- Find a book about selling and read it.
- You will not get rich overnight. Be patient and avoid scammers.
- Do not sell popular and expensive items as a new seller.

Many eBay sellers start by selling some of the things they do not use around their home—and not without a good reason. These items are usually in perfect condition and they are more likely to bring in more money if you sell them on eBay compared to a garage sale. Almost everyone has items around the house that they do not need—all they do is eat up space and gather dust. Selling them on eBay is a great way test the waters. If you do not have items lying around your home to sell, start with something that you know well. Look for items that have demand; something that people are buying. Avoid selling only what you like or the coolest, trendiest things you can find. You need to sell what the buyers want so you can make a profit. For any item you consider selling, do an eBay search to see how many people are selling the same and whether it is on sale. If there are too many sellers, maybe reconsider. If there is no seller offering what you want to sell, do a little research and see if it because nobody wants to buy it, or it is just because no other seller has thought of selling it. When too many sellers are offering a product, check the biddings to find out how strong the market is.

- Issues to Consider
- Cost: cost does not just mean the price of the item. Factor in additional expenses like how much it will cost to ship the item to you.
- Storage: is there room around your home to store the item safely as you wait for a buyer? Shipping: after a customer buys your item, how will you ship it to the buyer? Factor in the cost and labor issues. Extremely heavy, usually shaped or fragile items can be challenging to ship. Product life cycle: for how long will your item be in demand? Some items may be in high demand today but become very hard to sell the next day. Season: before you start selling an item, consider what time of the year it is. You cannot sell sweaters and heavy coats during summer, for instance.
- Where to Find What to Sell

Your home: search thoroughly around your home for things you no longer use. Check the garage, attic and closet. Flea markets: these can be an awesome source of items that will sell very well on eBay. Yard and garage sales: spend some time every week buying merchandise from garage sales. You will find many items that will sell on eBay for way more than you paid for them. Estate sales: you may not have much luck if a professional is handling the sale. However, you can purchase entire estates then pick and choose what to sell on eBay. Established retailers: find a store that needs to move products that are not selling. Discount stores: this will be very profitable especially if you buy out of season and wait until the items are in demand. Friends and family: ask the people you know if they have things that they would like to give away. When you become a seasoned eBay seller, you can start buying your merchandise from wholesalers. Selling things online is way easier than doing a yard sale. However, you still have a decision to make between Amazon and eBay. Everyone seemed to use this company about 10 years ago, but it has since kind of lost its flavor. Over the recent past, it seems to be making a few improvements and snapping up reputable companies. How does it make money? PayPal must be the first answer here. It is profitable for eBay and contributed to almost half of their revenue in 2014. Back to comparing it with Amazon. When eBay was the deal years ago, they charged an insertion fee and when the item sold, a value fee. Currently, eBay gives every seller not less than 20 free listings. The final value fee is still there, though. They have tried to simplify their final value fee calculations; so, they only charge 10% of the sale price as the final value fee. Subscription packages are available for power sellers. For a monthly fee, they get 150 to 2500 free listings, lower final value fees and a lower insertion fee (conditional). Sellers can also list their items or upgrade existing listings at a fixed price. Fixed price listings and auction listings attract the same fees and they both take advantage of customers who need to buy an item urgently. The fee structure for Amazon is more complex than eBay's. Amazon, sellers have two options: either list as Professionals or as an Individuals. Individuals attract $0.99 listing fee per item and a referral fee (6% to 45% depending on category). In addition, you are charged a variable closing fee (not variable for video, DVD, books and media, you will pay $1.35 per item). A seller can list their products in 20 to 30 different categories. Amazon sets and collects the shipping rates for BMDV (books, media, DVD, video). Buyers love BMDV categories because the total fee is easily calculated without checking the shipping rates of the seller. Payment is done via bank transfers and the Amazon's Fraud Protection service offers protection to sellers. eBay's selling fees used to be expensive and complicated but ever since they streamlined their fees on May 1st, the structure is easy and looks simple. Amazon, on the other hand, can be frustrating and confusing. It would be easy to show this using sample calculations but for both sites, structures and fees vary by category, payment option, and item weight. Choosing Amazon over eBay has some advantages. First, the site makes the buyer feel as if he is buying from Amazon directly. There is the "1-click buying" option and you can complete a transaction without leaving the site. A seller can also choose to have his products stored and shipped from Amazon's warehouses. A seller may choose eBay over Amazon because, then, he or she can personalize and customize listings. Also make listings more appealing and attract potential buyers. eBay has a new Valet service that gives sellers the option to have their products listed and even sold by eBay. The two companies have seller protection services and a way to contact the buyer should an issue arise. Setting up a seller's account on eBay is easier than it is on Amazon while the payment process is better on Amazon. A panel of experts chose to unravel 51 tips to help you become a successful seller on eBay.

Do Your Homework

1. Pick a day and take the time to explore the eBay site.
2. Acquire step-by-step guidance. www.ebay.com/education is a helpful place.

What to Sell?

1. Start with what you know.

1. Be keen and observant. Take advantage of opportunities to buy items.

1. Avoid starting out with a single product or product line. Try two and cross promote them.

1. Explore other categories to know what is hot. Check out www.ebay.com/sellercentral.

1. Try being a trading assistant.

1. Do not be too careful and take calculated risks occasionally.

1. Of you are selling something you are not familiar with, do not write a description before educating yourself.

1. Become a verified eBay member.

1. Be wise when choosing your eBay user ID. Let it be identifiable with what you are selling and descriptive.

1. Have a different user ID for your business.

1. Be organized in everything.

1. Have a designated photography area in your business location.

1. Take outstanding photos of your items.

Create Your Listing

1. HTML format looks more professional.

1. Avoid all capital letters in your title.

1. In your listings, give a specific and complete item description. Include many detailed photos.

1. Clearly outline your terms and conditions and warranty, guarantee, returns and shipping policies.

1. Create a listing schedule.

1. If you are an advanced user, try the seller's assistant pro service.

While You Are Selling

1. Feed the frenzy. To feed a bidding frenzy, set no reserve and a low opening bid prize.

1. Avoid getting stuck in a rut.

1. Just because your items are selling a lot does not mean that you are making profits. Evaluate.

1. As soon as you are notified of a sold item, respond with eBay's checkout system.

1. Arrange shipping immediately, once the buyer makes a payment.

1. Set reasonable handling and shipping costs.

1. Have regular shipping days.

1. Save time with the postage service from PayPal.

1. Use the USPS web site to schedule courier pickups.

1. Track a package to ensure its delivery.

Customers First

1. Always give punctual, courteous and prompt responses to your customers' questions.

1. Always remember the customer is king.

1. Give customers the same treatment that you would give guests in your house.

1. Remove roadblocks that may hinder buyers from buying your products such as not accepting a PayPal payment.

1. Respond quickly to buyers' emails.

1. Set aside time to post feedback.

1. Avoid being emotional while posting feedback.

Money Matters

1. Keep your books in order using accounting software.

1. Have a business or premium PayPal account.

1. Keep track of your expenses.

1. Use eBay keywords once you have settled.

1. Monitor your competition.

1. Sometimes, hold some items and wait until your competition sells out.

1. Nurture your customer database.

1. Cross-promote using your email signature.

1. Open an eBay store only after you have completed several transactions.

1. Take advantage of cross-promotion tools if you have an eBay store.

1. Use services like Endicia when you become a PowerSeller.

1. Do not just target buyers in the USA.

1. Only accept US dollars when selling to non-USA buyers.

Sometimes eBay sellers and buyers commit trading violations in their attempts to change the outcome of a sale or an auction. A good number of these violations are not seller exclusive or buyer exclusive—they apply to both. The nature of the violation does not matter; this kind of bad behavior affects every member of the eBay community. As a treasured member of that community, you have a responsibility of looking out for these violations to ensure that eBay remains a safe venue where people can conduct their business. If you notice a violation, do not be afraid of notifying the eBay Security Center. Unluckily, you may sometimes come across sellers who are not community-minded, and they may try to interfere with your sales or auctions. This interference can come in several forms, for instance, a seller may try to "steal" bidders or drive up bids illegally. Shill bidding: you are not allowed to place a bid on an auction with the intention of artificially inflating the final value. This undermines the trust of the community. Shill bidding is a serious issue and may violate the Federal wire fraud laws. It is a felony and you do not want to play around with it. Shill bidding has always been a part of auctions. To avoid being suspected of shill bidding, family members sharing the same computer and people who live together should not bid on one another's items. It is not that difficult to spot shill bidders, even for users that are not conversant with IP addresses and other technical stuff. If you check the auction history of a bidder, you will be able to determine their bidding pattern. It is suspicious when one keeps on bidding but never wins. Transaction interference: you may receive an email from a seller on eBay offering to sell you an item, like the one you are bidding on, for a cheaper price. This is what is known as transaction interference. It can hinder sellers from getting the highest possible bid. Transaction interception: an eBay scalawag can monitor the closing auctions and when they are over, they email the winner pretending to be the seller. They skillfully craft the email, making it look authentic and ask for payment. This is more than just trading violation; it is stealing. Fee avoidance or circumvention: this is where people go around the system to avoid paying eBay fees. There are so many ways in which an eBay user can commit this violation—sometimes, they do not even realize it: Avoid using the contact information of an eBay member to try and sell them a listed item off the eBay site. If a reserve price for an auction item was not met, do not use the contact information of a buyer to try and sell them the item off the site. Do not prematurely close an auction so you can privately sell it to someone who has offered a higher price via email. You can only sell unsuccessful bidders duplicates of the auction item through the Second Option. Excessive shipping charges: the handling and shipping fees that you charge must be reasonable. They should not be disproportionate to the item. Non-selling seller: when someone wins an auction, you cannot refuse payment and fail to complete the transaction.

Chapter 11

Facebook Marketing

Running a Facebook business page is one of the most feasible options you can use, but a challenge to many. You need to understand the platform first to guarantee success. If you are not sure where to start, here are the ten top things you need to know beforehand. First, you need to know why you are on Facebook in the first place, what you need to get from it and whom you are targeting. Besides, you also need to understand how to achieve what you are looking for in your pursuit. Cross promotion involves linking your page to other social networks, business cards and anywhere else where you can get as many eyes online to find your business. Share your personal profile with as many people as possible and get the word out. Make sure to invest in your page if you want to get a positive result from it. Whether it is going for sponsored stories, Facebook ads, offers, promoted posts, anything that you can invest into for a positive outcome, go for it. Ensure you offer value to your visitors, along with your objective. It is advisable keeping the content valuable and worthwhile. Then promotional marketers and sponsors can see the quality you provide. One thing is that only about 16% of your fans can see your post. To change this, you can use Facebook EdgeRank to determine what post appears on your newsfeed. If you want to take the efficiency of your posts to a completely new level, then this app is for you. Apart from the EdgeRank, Facebook has other features that you can make excellent use of as well. Such features include pinned posts, featured links, post targeting highlighted posts, custom tabs, and post scheduler, to mention but a few. These features can be far reaching in effect when it comes to making your posts stand out. If you use the space offered wisely, you can create a lasting impression on your visitors and make them want to come back continuously. This applies to the cover image, the about section and the other important factors you need to address in the space offered. This section gives you the opportunity to communicate your purpose and engage your visitors. The first thing a visitor is likely to see upon landing on your Facebook page is your cover photo. As such, you need to make sure this image talks details about your business, which can help the target group associate easily with your page. If you do not post regularly, then your page's visitors are likely to stop coming back. On the contrary, posting quite often keeps the communication going and the link with your visitors alive. However, it is wise ensuring that you are posting relevant information too. Make sure you have something that builds your audience, educates them and entertainment from time to time is worthwhile. Comments may seem to be a regular thing, and quite often than not, many people do not consider responding to them. This is one area where you can build your business page to levels you could not expect. Response to comments is essential as it keeps you in touch with your visitors, and, above all, helps understand what they expect of you. Also, keep your permissions open for visitors to get in touch. It may sound easy, but it takes commitment to make your Facebook business page what you want it to be. These ideas can help you get things started, just go for what works best for you. In the wake of online marketing, Facebook has been one of the avenues where you can market effectively. However, this calls for considering several things even before testing the waters. The most important barrier is competition, whether weak or strong. This can help understand reasons for failures or success on the Facebook platform. Besides this aspect, you also need to keep an eye on the following factors as well; these eight tips will take you to the top. One of the things that determine your success in Facebook is the reach you achieve with every single post. Once you post, people who have like or followed your page will see it, but this also depends on other factors as well. Above all, the best timing helps you gain an edge over the competition since others are also posting throughout the day and night. The best time to post is usually during the day when people can see what you have to offer. Not all posts perform the same, as some are more effective than others. Some of the best posts to go for include questions, videos, links, image posts, giveaways, coupons, and discounts. These posts add value but knowing what to post adds value and provides added benefit in enhancing your success. Most of the time, you need to ensure that the relevant posts on your wall are viewed by as many people as possible. In this case, posting on Sundays has been proposed as the way to go. If you are not able to post on a Sunday, Saturday is also a good day to post. If you are using a linking strategy on Facebook to articles on your website, then you are on the right track. However, you also need to consider the length of the article you are linking too. BuzzSumo recommends using 1,000 to 2,000-word articles, as they receive more interactions than the shorter ones. Anywhere between 3,000 and 4,000 also works wonders, so that is a great option for you as well. While people will visit your page to see what you have for the day, it does not mean they come there to spend all day. This calls for shunning long descriptions and going for the shorter ones, about 50 characters at most. If you have a 10-word description, you are good to go. It is not advisable to post this type of videos on Facebook. Instead, you can opt for embedding a video or directly upload it. In case you have published a video post on your page, go a step further and upload its source on Facebook. With its versatility, Facebook works well with other social media sites; Instagram is one of these options. You can merge them so that whenever you post a picture, it is uploaded to your Facebook account. It is easier and more efficient as well. Another great tool to enhance your Facebook by boosting the engagement you get. Including them in your posts can go a long way in offering results you did not expect.

Thoughtful ideas that can enhance your effectiveness on this platform, if well approached; this is a great way of enhancing your Facebook marketing. Once you have your Facebook page up and ready, what you post there is as important as the page itself. Therefore, you must go an extra mile to ensure you have the right posts that will keep your visitors coming back for more every day. This means knowing what your business audience needs and what the clients are expecting of you. Whenever you are posting on your page, you should ensure you have a clear objective behind the necessity to communicate. Start by analyzing what you want to get from a post, as this is reliable in making it more efficient. Remember, the goal of your post should be apparent. There are many ways you can use a post to engage your visitors. You can ask a question, or post a photo and let them caption, leave a blank for them to fill in and many other ways as well. The best thing here is to draw them closer. Just make it short, but ensure it is compelling enough. Using a concise yet compelling language and or image, but keep vague or deceptive language at bay, if you want to generate clicks, a little professionalism can work out best for you. Posting photos have been known to receive more attention over word posts but posting a link has been found to outperform the photos. Therefore, combining both a photo post and link can be more efficient. Just ensure that the page where the link leads has a big picture that will appear along with a short description of the post. If this is not the case, then you can just paste a photo and a brief link to go with it.

One of the things your visitors will keep coming back is if they find inspiration in your posts. As such, this aspect is one of the essential things you cannot afford to leave out in your post. All you need to do here is ensure your sentiments are authentic enough. You can use memes, quotes that your audience can relate with and inspirational photos if you want to enhance shares. An excellent post does not have to be promotional always. Your Facebook is not an advertisement billboard. Therefore, although you will need to do promotions and offers from time to time, it is wise to ensure you are not over doing it. Consider providing helpful content for your audience apart from just promotions. Going for a mixture of the two can go a long way in making things work out best. A well-crafted post can attract visitors and keep the existing followers. It is thus advisable to utilize the effectiveness of this factor to ensure you make the best out of every single post. Make every post count. Most of the time, people do not take Facebook business pages as seriously as they should. As a result, many end up making mistakes that cost them negative effects and reviews. If you are running a business page on this platform, then ensure you keep these mistakes at bay.

1. Making it about you

This is the first misconception. Many will think that their business page on Facebook is about them, but the opposite is the case. This page should be more about your visitors; you should keep them in mind and only post about yourself occasionally.

2. Sweating the details

One of the things you need to avoid is making your page boring by posting almost every other minute. No matter how great your posts are, just posting in a one out of ten ration goes a long way in communicating to your visitors. You do not have to flood them with dame information repeatedly to let them know what you have, just take it slow.

3. Running a dormant page

This mistake also goes unnoticed and can be devastating. If you are not ready to manage the page, do not start it until you are sure you can post continuously. This means ensuring you post regularly, not just once a month and you disappear.

4. You are not social

The word speaks volumes; social media is about being social. If you fail in this aspect, then you have just lost. Being social includes keeping in touch with your visitors by giving them content, engaging them and responding to their comment too. Maintain the connection, and you will have engaging eyes coming back for more.

5. Insufficient linking

The Facebook business page cannot efficiently perform if you do not link it appropriately. You need to ensure you keep it connected to other sources where visitors can get detailed information on some matters. Keeping your page locked out of the outside world will only do it more harm than good.

6. Creating the wrong impression

The perception your visitor will have about you and your business depends on the first impression they get from you. This relies on the cover image you put on your page. If the photo does not positively or concisely represent your business, then you may lose potential customers or readers.

7. Poor timing

Lack of proper timing to get your audience can cost you. You need to analyze your prospective visitors and identify the best time they are likely to see your posts. This helps earn a level of certainty that your point is getting to the intended audience. It is advisable that you post during weekends, especially if you are targeting consumers.

8. Too much professional approach

This being a business page does not mean you go in with a clenched formal approach. This will likely be perceived as inaccessible, which can dent your connection with visitors. It is wise you post slowly on the professional approach and embrace a personality approach so that others can relate to you easily. These mistakes may appear ineffective, but they can be devastating if two or more affect your business page. Therefore, you need to ensure you keep them in check to keep your page's performance at its best. Creating a Facebook page is one thing but making it a successful one is another thing altogether. If you are looking to make your page stand out, then you need to include these four simple steps. One essential thing to keep an eye on here is your ideal client. The idea behind knowing your prospective visitors helps utilize your space well to put the right information in the right section, where it can be clearly seen. Going for niche marketing and segmentation is also far reaching in page success, as this enhances focusing on your target audience. Remember, the more you narrow down, the better. If you want to make your page look like a website you brought right into Facebook, then the way you brand is the secret. This helps you bridge Facebook to your sites, although you do not have to rush your clients through Facebook. Avoid creating more clicks for your visitors to get to your site, as this may work against what you intended to achieve. If there is one formula that is usually underrated by most business owners, then it is inbound marketing. The fact is that marketing tactics are essential for the success of any intention to bring traffic to your doorstep, and Facebook is no different. Primarily, this strategy has to do with using keywords, videos, opt-in opportunities as well as cross-promotions. You need to ensure you have great content on your FB page as you would with a website or blog. The good news is that there are apps like Networked Blog that you can use to link this content and beef up your Facebook page. The best thing you can do for your page is to be committed efficiently, and this means real-time engagement. This means acting whenever necessary for time and effort to materialize. As such, you need to keep coming back to your page and check out the interests, likes, opinions from your visitors and other important things. The best thing to remember here is the fact that engagement is all about doing it for your fans than for yourself. To achieve this, ensure your posts are more about your fans and give them an opportunity to talk about themselves. Coming up with a successful Facebook page is never the easiest thing to do, but it does not have to freak you out, nevertheless. Knowing what to do and why you need to have it done is the first step in realizing this essential aspect. Therefore, understanding what is expected of you can go a long way in preparing you to tackle the task efficiently. This can necessitate checking out other

Facebook pages to get an idea of what you need to do. After that, commitment and sacrificing your time to tend to your page comes in handy. Above all, remember to make it more about your fans than yourself. Facebook is the leading social media site with many users who daily log into their counts. People connect with their friends' online and share on the life progress on various issues. Facebook marketing is a new trend where people purchase items from advertised Facebook posts. The following are ways in which one can market items online on Facebook; There are no fees charged for creating a Facebook account. A Facebook page enables a business to identify itself through sharing images, links, and posts. A customized Facebook page gives customers a better grasp of the kind services and goods offered. Unlike Facebook accounts, pages do not have a limitation on the number of friends. Additionally, someone does not have to be your friend to like your posts. Online marketing can efficiently be as simple as placing advertisements on a Facebook page. The advertisements come on the side of a Facebook page. It includes a picture of the item on sale in addition to the link or hyperlink to a business page. You can customize each advertisement to meet a specific group of users or for a certain location. Holding various Facebook contests on items and rewarding participants is a great awareness creation tool. Many people get to know your brands through such contests. The contests will direct users in participation on a third party already established application. Sponsored posts are a kind of advertisement where a user gets to share the experience with the certain product. If someone went for snacks at McDonald's, their friends can easily get to learn of their experience. In this way, products are promoted and get more users. Sponsored stories are the only advertisement available on the mobile devices. Once a user likes a certain business page, the information is automatically posted on the news feed. A brand gets more fans through sponsored stories. Facebook Open graph is unlike the other advertising tools where one just likes or comments on a specific story; an open graph creates interactivity between the users and the seller. The third-party application enables the actions that users perform on Facebook posts. Entrepreneurs need creativity in deciding the kind of action users can take such as listen or read. Facebook Exchange allows retailers to get a chance of placing real-time bidding. Through the exchange tool, a retailer can create re-advertise a post when a retailer visits and fails to make a purchase. The advertisements used to appear in the side column but currently appear on the news feed. These tools are great in carrying out marketing on the Facebook site. Through these tools, a business gains the much-needed publicity. All social media platforms provide an opportunity for creating advertisements. Still, Facebook is the best site in terms of features, insights, and audience. Facebook is an ideal place for a business to start from. Many businesses end up misusing their resources when Facebook ads become ineffective. It is vital to have knowledge of the way Facebook works and its best practices. Facebook offers insights into the kind of business that generates revenues and best-selling products. The insights are integral in the determination of whether a product is worth the effort. The publisher will learn the specifics on an audience before spending money while targeting them. The Facebook insights work through mining data from the people who have liked your Facebook page and showing their preferences on your products. It saves time and money on advertising according to customer's desires. Every audience is unique, especially when dealing with a variety of products. You can select two advertisements or more depending on your targeted audience. Still, the same ad can be sent to two different audiences. For example, when dealing with clothing, you can target individual persons as well as entrepreneurs who will consider buying in bulk. Before placing the Facebook, advertisements ensure that you have a business Facebook page. It allows users to be familiarized with your product before placing in any marketing tactic. Also, Facebook advertisements allow hyperlinking. The advert should lead people to the page to learn more on the product. Before placing any advertisement, ensure there are likes on your Facebook page. This way, you will not spend money on an advertisement without a set clientele that you are targeting. Striking advertisements are important for drawing attention to your Facebook ad. Many people major in how to create the advertisement with no mention of the image. Visual attraction is important. Hire an expert to create the advertisement if you cannot do it. Facebook indicates that you cannot use images that contain more than twenty words. Limit the text used. Images will attract attention to your advertisement. Before developing an advertisement setup, a bid strategy. A budget is needful to avoid overspending. Optimized CPM allows you to put together a budget and strategy. This tool develops an advertisement based on the constraints and goals provided. Until you are well versed with the cost of space on Facebook, let Facebook develop the advertisement for you to minimize overspending. Creation of a killer Facebook advertising is based on understanding the platform and maximizing on the features. As much as the advertisement is important, the platform used is important. Create a Facebook page and build on it. Still, keep in mind that technology is changing. Familiarize yourself with changing features.

Chapter 12

Ecommerce Secrets

People are buying less from brick-and-mortar stores. The ecommerce industry is growing rapidly. Although the growth is massive and offers countless opportunities for ecommerce entrepreneurs, a ton of newbies keep on making mistakes that prevent them from being successful. One expert in this industry pointed out that the profitability of your online store does not just depend on an awesome website and a quality product. These are just essentials that every other ecommerce online store will have. This expert goes on to give you the essentials that will make a difference in your business and set you apart from the rest.

A Pre-Launch Audience

A very high percentage of entrepreneurs start marketing after they have launched their store. The issue with this approach is that online marketing efforts do not deliver instant results. During this time, you will still be required to pay hosting fees among other expenses. Rather than wait, establish a pre-launch audience. Even if your product is neither original nor new, spread the word. Use email list sign ups, product giveaways and social media.

Customer Lifetime Value

It is not easy to convert customers. The conversion rate in most cases is only 1-3%. Therefore, every sale must count. This means that you should focus on the CLV (customer lifetime value). Make sure that the customer has an amazing experience during their first purchase. On top of that, follow up. Email marketing will help with this. Reach out for special seasons and holidays too.

The Power of Remarketing

Ecommerce professionals spent a huge amount of money on marketing. The goal is to attract new customers who will hopefully make a purchase. However, many of these professionals forget about the shoppers they have already convinced. There is a very high chance of repeat customers buying from your store again and even spending more cash. Make sure to target those who have already bought from you. Use AdWords and Facebook campaigns to your advantage.

Let the Customers Do the Talking

As an entrepreneur you must create a strong brand identity. It allows you to establish an emotional connection with potential buyers. A strong relationship with your passionate customers may help you leverage their enthusiasm. They will advertise your store through word of mouth. Most marketing methods are neither effective nor trusted. Nonetheless, you need to know that even your best customers will not decide to market your business on their own. You need to offer them motivation. Ask them for input on your service or product. To build this enthusiasm among customers, hold social media contests. If you work hard to personalize the interactions, your customers will be more prompted to be true ambassadors.

If You Opt for Dropshipping, Do Not Botch It

Dropshipping makes sales simpler for ecommerce professionals. But that does not mean that it does not have its downsides. Issues like low-quality products, slow delivery, among others can kill your business. Therefore, do your due diligence and partner with reliable suppliers and shipping companies.

Chapter 13
Mistakes People Make Dropshipping

It is not rare to see a promising online store fall apart just a few months after being launched. If you are an ecommerce entrepreneur, you may have experienced failure yourself. Most of these failures occur in dropshipping. Dropshipping can bring huge success to your ecommerce business when done correctly. It is preferred because the seller does not have to stock goods themselves. This model can make your business run smoothly. However, a few routine mistakes will make you miss out on the benefits. For those starting out your own dropshipping stores, here are the common errors to avoid.

Selecting the Wrong Supplier

Picking out a supplier is almost as crucial as picking a niche. The supplier influences everything from the quality of the product to the delivery times. Make sure you go for someone who will offer what you are looking for. Check out testimonials and reviews from people who have worked with the supplier. In addition, place a test order. You will get a firsthand experience and know how the shipping process works. You will also know whether the product meets your standards.

Depending on a Single Vendor

Even after you get that amazing supplier, do not become complacent. He may run out of stock sometime when you have orders. Worse still, his business may fall apart. A problem like this could put you out of business too. Look for a backup supplier to help when the primary supplier cannot deliver. Your dropshipping business will continue to serve customers as usual. Before you do this, check your primary supplier's terms and conditions.

Surprise Shipping Fees

Are you completely honest about shipping fees when listing your product prices? Shoppers abandon their carts primarily because of high shipping costs. Surprise shipping costs, however, are worse since they show up at the end of checkout. Make your customers happy with clear shipping costs. A consistent flat rate would help, or better still, a "shipping calculator". Free shipping is powerful. Just make sure your margins are not hurt. 90% of shoppers are prompted to buy free shipping.

Lack of After-Purchase Tracking

When a customer makes a purchase, they will want to know when the order will be at their door. Nonetheless, some dropshippers think their work is done once the customer clicks "checkout". When you do not communicate with your customers, they may think they have been scammed. Offer them a tracking system for their orders—one that is easy to use. This communication will come in handy when an order is delayed.

Lackluster Returns

You cannot offer 100% customer satisfaction, no matter how much you try. Have a smooth return policy to avoid facing angry customers. The instructions should be clear and the responses timely. Your chances of surviving in this industry will be higher if you run several stores. When one store flops and you have already quit your job, you will have a plan B.

Chapter 14

First Profitable Product

A mong the challenges that new entrepreneurs face, is that of choosing an in-demand product to sell. Deciding on a product can be tricky. Everything you want to sell may already be in the market and you will face a lot of competition going forward. Fortunately, there are still opportunities that you can exploit. Here are practical steps to help you find the perfect product. You can never go wrong with solving the pain of a customer. Tylenol is successful because it solves people's headache issues. What common frustration do you notice, especially with existing product lines? When someone is enthusiastic about a certain hobby or trade, they are more likely to spend a great amount for exactly what they are looking for. Having hobbyists as customers will also give you the added advantage of loyalty and high engagement. Picking a niche just because you are passionate about it can be risky. However, you can use your skills to come up with a unique product. Do you know so much about an industry from working there? The skills you have acquired can make your skill set outstanding. Use your expertise to create an online business. Noticing a trend in advance can prove useful. You will be able to make a name for yourself in the market before other sellers do. Be careful not to confuse a trend with a fad. Customer reviews can give you so much insight. What customers are saying can inspire your next product or service. Look specifically for complaints and shortcomings. Search engines' organic traffic is a crucial marketing channel. What are people searching for and how frequently do they search for it? You need to understand SEO and keyword research for this method. Testing the market is the best way to know whether you are onto something. Launch the product with a small investment and see how it goes. Initial interest (or lack of it) will tell you a lot. Check out sites such as eBay, Amazon, and Etsy. Categories such as "Most wished for" and "What's hot" show what customers currently want. Use a tool such as Jungle Scout for more information. Low overhead products are low risk compared to those that are expensive to produce. In your final price, you must factor in the production, holding, shipping, and marketing costs. If you already have a category or industry that you are interested in, look for related items that people buy together. Amazon displays this information. Always keep an open mind. New ideas are constantly popping up and you need to be alert.

Chapter 15
Online Store Name

A powerful brand name will give you an advantage when starting out. As a matter of fact, the right name may be your most important asset while the wrong one may end up costing millions in lost profits. Take the process of choosing a name very seriously so your store can stand out. To help you with this decision, here are useful pointers. A short, snappy brand name has a few advantages; it's easy to remember and pronounce. Additionally, it will fit in the header of the homepage. Every day, there are thousands of new brands being launched. Because of this, the name you come up with may already be taken. It is not easy to come up with a compelling name that is also unique. However, there are strategies that you can employ: Combine different short words. Even better, choose words that rhyme such as "Snack Shack". Tweak an existing word or create a new one. Skype, eBay and Google are all prominent names and they are not even real words. Try something personal. A pet name, nickname, or your name may work. Research your direct competitors to see their names then sit down and think of a different name. The challenge is finding a name that relates to your niche and products while being different from the names of your competitors. After coming up with a few name options, it is time to check the domain (.com is recommended) availability. Most people always go for .com so this may be difficult. Do not be obsessed with chasing the mythical perfect name. Just be sure to choose a solid one. You may want to sell on other platforms as well such as Etsy, eBay, or Amazon. Even if you do not plan on doing it, check the names you have chosen on popular sites. You do not want customers to confuse your business. Do not worry if your domain name is already taken. You can opt for another TLD. When your business picks up, you can then buy .com. Alternatively, modify the domain name by combining the name of the product with the brand name or adding something creative. Make sure your name idea is not legally protected. If you are in the U.S, check out The United States Patent and Trademark Office. The database is free. For Canadians, check the Canadian Intellectual Property Office website. If you cannot think of names, think about themes. Observe yourself, conduct a survey, and listen to people around you.

Examples of Catchy Business Names

Death Wish Coffee: this one tells you that the coffee is strong. The Sock Market: from the name, you can tell that this is your go-to socks store. United by Blue: this is not just a brand; it is a movement that protects the waterways and oceans. The store sells outdoor products.

Chapter 16

Dropshipping Pricing Strategies

Dropship resellers always struggle when it comes to pricing products on their ecommerce sites. Lucky for you, there are several pricing strategies for dropshipping that you can use. Your approach will depend on your business model, supplier, and products. Some experts may argue that your pricing strategy should be constantly changing as you try different things to see what works. It does not matter whether you believe this or not; picking a dropshipping strategy is a crucial step when launching your dropshipping business. The first consideration is the type of product you plan to sell. Electronics, for instance, sell in high volumes but with a lower margin. Home décor and fragrances, on the other hand, sell in lower volumes but with a high margin. You should pick a niche first so you can think about a pricing strategy. The next step is discussing with your supplier. Send the (support desk or sales representative) an email asking for price setting recommendations. Even if they do not give much advice initially, establishing a good relationship with them may help you get useful advice. Check out the following popular pricing strategies. Fixed markup cost is attained by taking the product cost and adding a pre-set profit margin. Use either a fixed percentage markup or fixed dollar markup. When choosing between the two, consider the average cost of the merchandise. If you are a dollar store supplier or you sell cheap phone accessories, the best approach is the fixed dollar markup. Tiered markup cost is solid when your supplier sells a wide variety of products with high and low dollar values. It is ideal if you want to make enough with your low-cost items and at the same time, not price the expensive ones too high. Set levels/tiers for your products such that those below $10 have a higher markup (maybe 50%) and the $200-$500 items have a lower markup (maybe 15%). There is no limit for the number of tiers you can set. Setting the price as "discount" or mark down from the MSRP (Manufacturer's Suggested Retail Price) is a common approach. Offering, say a 20% discount, will win you customers who want to save. Before picking your discount, assess the competition and product types.

MSRP (Manufacturer's Suggested Retail Price)

Small-scale retailers commonly use this approach to maintain a decent profit while avoiding price wars at the same time. Using the suggested retail price keeps the retailer from making the decision. This is a great approach but if you do not offer a discount, you will not have an advantage over your competition. Psychological pricing is set such that the customer thinks they are buying at a cheap price. Odd pricing is the most common tactic. The set price ends in cents and in odd numbers such as 5,7 and 9. When the price is set at $9.95, the customer rounds it up to $9 and not $10.

Chapter 17
Store Rank in Search Engines

Nothing gives new storeowners a headache like SEO (search engine optimization) when it comes to digital marketing. There are tools to help with this, but the technical knowledge does not come easily to most people. This chapter aims at helping you get started with SEO. Setup recommended tools such as Google Analytics and Google Search Console. Create a Google Search Console account and submit your sitemap. Your Shopify store generates a sitemap file automatically and lists the individual pages of your website. Check for crawling errors using Google Search Console. A crawling error occurs when a bot fails to reach certain pages. Always fix these errors as soon as you receive the alert. Google Keyword's Planner will help you get keyword ideas and determine keywords' search volume. Different pages on your website may rank for different keywords. Proper keyword research will help you know what pages you are supposed to create.

Page Optimizations

Only use a single H1 tag on pages. These tags act as the key headline and contain the main keywords of the page. Do not manually add another one on the page. Page titles should not exceed 60 characters. Google rarely displays more than 50-60 characters of the page title. Ensure that your main keywords are at the beginning or near the beginning of the title. The meta description should be short and punchy. Keep it under 155 characters. Page titles should be compelling and human-readable. Make the title interesting and include keywords. Your page URL should have a keyword. For Shopify storeowners, the page title is the URL by default. Include descriptive filenames and alt tags in images. Have a link building strategy. Google and other search engines use the relevancy, quality, and number of links as a factor for ranking. Analyze the earned links and mentions of your competitors. Use sites such as Ahrefs Site Explorer and Moz's Link Explorer to see which sites are linking to competitors. Look for press mentions opportunities. Create a basic strategy for content marketing. A comprehensive content strategy requires a lot of time, but you can start with a simple one by:

- Brainstorming customer questions.
- Offering customers more value (example, simple guide articles).
- Using keywords that match their questions.

Blog posts and informational articles should be at least 500 words. The content should be clear and to the point. Your product descriptions should be original. Product pages should at least have product reviews. Redirect when necessary. Make use of platforms such as Pinterest, Instagram, Twitter, and Facebook. Build your brand and protect your identity. See how your site looks on mobile. Your site should be fast. Check out Google's recommended practices if you are unsure about something. Keep up with changes. Read Think with Google and Webmaster Central publications to get updates directly from Google. Above all else, the most effective SEO strategy is catering to searches.

Chapter 18
Product Descriptions That Sell

A product description can be defined as a marketing copy defining a product and explaining why it is worth buying. It offers customers necessary information concerning the features, specifications, and benefits of the said products. Its purpose is to compel a customer to purchase. However, marketers and entrepreneurs make one common mistake when coming up with this copy. They focus solely on describing the products. This is wrong because a product description is not just an information dispenser for search engines—it is supposed to convince real people. So then, how do you convince your site visitors using your product descriptions? Without an ideal buyer in mind when writing a product description, you will just splash words that address no one. You need to address the target audience in a personal and direct way. Go as far as asking and answering questions as though they are sitting right there with you. Always use the second person "you". It is normal to get excited about what you are selling. However, you should know that customers do not care that much about the details. Their main interest is how they will benefit from your product. Is it going to address their problem? How? Sell the experience. Here is an example of a yeah, yeah phrase "excellent product quality". The customer will think, "yeah, yeah, sure." After all, that is what every seller says, right? Avoid these phrases by being specific. Instead of mentioning quality directly, use features that portray quality. Superlatives barely come off as sincere. You must prove, clearly, why you consider your product the most advanced, easiest or the best. Give proof and be specific. If you cannot do this, tone the description down.

Alternatively, quote customers who think your product is the best. According to science, the desire to own something increase when the person holds it in their hands. As an online seller, customers cannot even touch your products. In addition to quality videos and photos, there is another trick: let the potential buyer imagine the experience of owning the product. Start a sentence with imagine then continue to explain the experience. Mini stories make the reader forget that you are trying to sell to them. Talk about the inspiration behind the product, the testing process, etc. Sensory words engage extra brain power and increase sales. Words like smooth, velvety, crunchy, bright, and crisp can go a long way. In most cases, customers opt for the product with many positive reviews. However, you can subtly include social proof in your reviews. Even better, include the photo of the person who gave the comment. Your web design should encourage web visitors to go through the product descriptions. Make the design clear and scannable so it can appeal to readers.

Chapter 19
DIY Guide to Product Photography

A potential customer will judge your brand and products based on how you visually represent your items. This means that your photos should be beautiful and of high-quality. For new store owners, a professional photography studio can be a little costly. DIY product photography is the perfect alternative. You can take compelling photos as long as you have the right tools and use proper techniques. The technique outlined below is referred to as The Window Light Technique. It is the best for those on a budget. It is a simple technique aimed at producing high-quality photos. The gear you use will greatly impact your photography. This is an issue that can be confusing to newcomers. High-end gadgets are not necessary. The only costly thing is probably the camera. A super expensive Nikon camera gives awesome results, but you can do without it. In fact, you can use your smartphone. The Canon G10 is modest but you can shoot outstanding photos with it. Start with what you have for now and see if the pictures are fine. The photo quality depends on more than just the camera. If you are working with a slow shutter camera and you hold it, you are likely to end up with blurry photos. That is why you need a tripod. There are many cheap options on Amazon—there is no need to spend too much. As a store owner, you may end up doing so many shoots. A white sweep is ideal because when it gets dirty, you can remove the dirty part. For an even cheaper option, buy a poster board at the local art or drug store. When buying, choose pure white. When using window light, one side of your object will be directly struck by light while the other side will be the shadow side. Bounce cards are used to reflect light onto the shadow.

The best material for bounce cards is foam board. Another tactic is using a black foam board to deepen the shadow. It is useful when both the background and the product are white. A regular folding table will work just fine. Clamps or tapes help to secure the board for a perfect sweep. A window or windows close to a wall make the best room. A big window will let in more light.

How to Take Photos of Your Product

- Set up the table: place it very close to the window and turn off lights in the room.
- Set up the sweep: the sweep should be vertical.
- Set up the camera: set the white balance to auto AWB. Turn the flash setting off then set the image settings to RAW or the largest JPG setting.
- Set up the product: place it at the center of the surface.
- Set up your reflector card: feel free to try different angles.
- Take the picture and evaluate it.
- Retouch your pictures.

Chapter 20

Grow Your Audience on Instagram

You want to regularly engage the audience you already have and get more followers. To engage your current followers, and post engaging photos. If you want more people to follow you, use the most popular hashtags. Some filters are more favored by Instagram users more than others. Use the preferred filters to make your followers more interested. These are the most popular filters:

- Normal (No Filter)
- Clarendon
- Juno
- Lark
- Ludwig
- Gingham
- Valencia
- X-Pro II
- Lo-Fi
- Amaro

The Right Times

Trial and error are the best approach here. What has worked before? What has not worked? The IconoSquare optimization section gives detailed information of your posting history and engagement. The report will also tell you the best times to post.

Look for your competitors' accounts on Instagram and engage with your audience. The fact that they follow that account means that they are interested in your products or products like yours.

- Follow them
- Like their photo
- Comment on their photo

Pay for Product Reviews and Sponsored Posts

This tactic may not be free, but it can yield amazing results when used properly. Create a list of powerful; accounts in your niche. They should have a large following and an email address somewhere in their profile. Ask them, via email, what they charge for sponsored posts. Tag your location (where the video/photo was taken or your current location). Locations have the advantage of a specified Instagram feed and Story. If you are a local business, this feature may be very useful for your business. Do not forget to engage with posts of people in the same location. When someone visits your Instagram profile, you have a few seconds to convince them to hit the follow button. The "Highlights" feature gives a quick idea of what your brand is about. Do not shy away from asking people to follow you. Promise more amazing content. Incorporate the request into your posts or captions. Give a hint of something exciting that is coming up. Be on the lookout for trending hashtags or topics and align your content with that. Take advantage of holidays. Find relevant conversations and contribute in a meaningful way. Having a user tag a friend under your post has several benefits. Running giveaways encourages followers to tag their friends who will, in turn, follow you. Publishing consistently entices new followers. When people land on your profile, they should be assured of regular exciting content. Use Social Blade (it is free) to see how your following is growing. If you run a Business account, you will have an Instagram Analytics dashboard. You will get free valuable insight. There are so many tools at your disposal for use in your Instagram strategy. Here are some of the most useful ones:

- Later
- IconoSquare

- Webstagram

Chapter 21
International Shipping

Shipping outside your country is worth considering if you want your ecommerce business to grow. This means that you must understand what shipping internationally entails. The first thing you need is a strategy that is ideal for you and your store. There is no perfect list of practices that suits all businesses. However, there are some central decisions that you should consider when building your strategy. Do you have a specific country and product in mind? If you are not sure, maybe these indicators will help. Start close and small. Ship close to home so you can know what the experience is like. Monitor current demand. Analyze your shop traffic to see the countries that are already showing interest. Consider the countries' main language. Expand to countries that speak the language(s) you are fluent in. Identify suitable non-domestic markets. Know which markets suit your business.

Country Rules and Regulations

Once you find suitable countries and products, check the rules and regulations. Some items are prohibited or limited in certain countries. Check that government's website or use UPS to get this information.

Shipping Internationally with Shopify Shipping

If you are a Shopify merchant in Canada and US, you can get discounted rates with Canada Post, DHL Express, UPS, and USPS. When choosing a shipping carrier, consider these four factors. Costs: using several carriers will help you save money. Delivery options: have your customers choose from a variety of delivery options with a tradeoff between price and timeline. Tracking and insurance: for more expensive packages, consider insurance. Transparency is crucial to any strategy. Be communicative and transparent with your buyers about shipping costs. If they get surprised at checkout, they are likely to abandon the cart. Make everything plain and clear in your policy. While determining the total price of the product, you should factor in the following:

- Cost of product
- Packaging
- Cost of shipping'
- Handling charges
- Duties and taxes
- Credit card fee
- Profit margin

As far as shipping is concerned, you will need boxes, maybe stuffing, or bubble wrap. The packaging should be simple but sturdy. Consider and compare using a rate calculator for your carriers of choice to determine the price for your average, smallest and largest order. Structure your pricing: determine whether you will use flat rate shipping, carrier rate shipping or free shipping. International packages are handled by many facilities before they get to the customer. The handling charge depends on how long it takes you to prepare the package. Be prepared to deal with additional taxes, duties and customs. Countries differ and it is upon you to make sure that the delivery is smooth. Customs: these are taxes or tariffs that a government levies on imported goods. Duties and taxes: these are tariffs or taxes imposed on international sale of goods. The percentage is usually not fixed.

Chapter 22

Marketing on Pinterest

P interest is not your conventional social platform. This chapter is meant to help you understand the network and how you can use it to reach your target audience. Pinterest is a platform where users, known as "pinners", can save pins containing images, descriptions and links onto various boards for future reference. The boards can either be public or private. A user can create their own pin by uploading links or images manually, finding a pin via search or just by stumbling upon one on their Pinterest feed. Pinterest is mainly for storing inspiration and ideas. There are over 250 million users on Pinterest. This may not match the number of users on other platforms, but it is still something, especially because Pinterest has exceptional selling power. People go to Pinterest to search for things to buy, not to scroll down aimlessly. Online stores with physical goods have a high chance of getting positive results on Pinterest. B2C companies also more likely to benefit compared to B2B. Statistically, women use Pinterest more than men. 70% of the users are women while 30% are men. However, more men are signing up on the platform. According to statistics offered by Pinterest, 40% of the households on the platform have an annual income of more than 100K. An effective Pinterest profile is the first step to successful marketing. Do not set up a personal account; open a business one for the store. This way, you will have access to advertising tools and Pinterest analytics. If you had already opened a personal account, it is possible to change it into a business account. Keep everything consistent with your other social media profiles as well as your website. The username and logo should be the same across all platforms. Click on the "Settings" options if you want to make changes to your profile. While editing, you will see a "Featured Boards" option. They will always be displayed above your other boards. Use them to showcase important content. There are a few reasons why organizing your boards is important. One is that you will win more followers if you categorize the boards into niche subsections. Use a different board for every type of product and audience section. You can also create boards within boards. Include keywords in your descriptions and use hashtags to squeeze in more keywords. Note: all pins should have a visual component and link to a relevant page).

- Product pins: these have videos/photos of a product and link to the purchase page.
- Content and blog posts
- Infographics
- Videos

Extra Tips

- Use several dominant colors to make your pins stand out.
- Do not use too much whitespace (keep it less than 30%).
- Make use of group boards.
- You can pay to have your pins promoted.

Conclusion

Dropshipping is a method of retail fulfillment where stores do not actually stock their products. When someone buys a product, the store buys it from another party and then ships it to the customer directly. The merchant neither handles nor sees the product. Dropshipping is different from the conventional retail model in that, in dropshipping the seller does not own an inventory. He or she purchases an order from a third party. The dropshipping model, like everything else, has drawbacks and benefits. You need less capital: this is arguably the biggest advantage. You do not need thousands of dollars to start an ecommerce store. Conventional retailers need to have a huge amount of capital to build their inventory. In dropshipping, you only purchase a product once a customer has placed an order and made the payment. An initial inventory investment is not needed. Easy to start: an ecommerce business becomes much easier to run when you do not handle physical products. You will not worry about a warehouse, packing and shipping, tracking inventory, handling returns, and much more. Low overhead: since you will not be dealing with a warehouse or purchasing inventory, expect low overhead expenses. A lot of people run a dropshipping businesses from their home office with their laptop and only use about $100 per month. The expenses may increase as your business grows but they will still be low. Flexible location: if you have an internet connection, you can manage your dropshipping business from anywhere. You only need to efficiently communicate with customers and suppliers. Wide variety pf products: the fact that you do not pre-purchase and stock products means that you can offer a wide variety of items to your buyers. List any item you want on your website whenever a supplier stock it. Easy to scale, when you are running a traditional business, the amount of work you need to do increases as the business grows. You can have a less painful growth process by having dropshipping suppliers process additional orders.

Disadvantages

Low margins: the dropshipping niche is competitive and low margins are a huge disadvantage. Starting the business is easy and there are low overhead costs. Because of this, multiple merchants can set shop then sell products at a throw-away price. These merchants may have poor customer service and low-quality websites, but customers will still compare prices. Cutthroat competition can damage the profit margin. The wise thing to do would be to explore a niche that is ideal for dropshipping. Inventory issues: when you stock products yourself, it is easy to know what is in or out of stock. The third-party merchants you are outsourcing from have other customers and inventory keeps on changing. Shipping complexities: shipping costs get complicated because your products are sourced from multiple suppliers. Supplier error: dropshipping suppliers are not perfect, regardless of how seasoned they are. If your supplier makes a mistake during fulfillment of an order, you must take responsibility. Sometimes, these suppliers may taint your reputation. When getting your dropshipping business off the ground, you must consider so many things. You can easily get overwhelmed and forget to prioritize the important ones. That is why you will find this list helpful. It clearly outlines the elements that will facilitate your business's success. Come up with a solid plan for adding value to potential customers. This is the success factor that matters most. It applies to all businesses and more so a dropshipping business. You will have to compete with a myriad of shops that are offering the same product. To stand out in the market, you need to make sure that you are not just selling a product; you are offering solutions, information, and insight. You are in the business of information as much as you are in the dropshipping business. How do you plan to solve problems and add value to customers? If you find yourself unable to answer this question, you may want to investigate another niche.

Focus on SEO and Marketing

Traffic on your site is the second most crucial ingredient for success. Lack of traffic on your site is a huge problem and can be a source of frustration. In as much as driving traffic and marketing is essential, it is not easy to outsource. Most small businesses cannot afford it and you may have to do it on your own. You will need to acquire guest posting, outreach, marketing, and SEO skills.

This will matter a lot when you are starting out and no one has an idea that your business exists. 75% of your time should be dedicated to marketing. For the complete newbies, here are some helpful resources.

SEO Resources

- SEOMoz
- SearchEngineLand
- SEOBook
- Distilled

Marketing Resources

- Hubspot Blog
- Seth Godin's Blog
- Burst Free Product Photos
- QuickSprout
- KissMetrics Blog
- SparringMind
- CopyBlogger
- Mixergy

Ecommerce Marketing Resources

- Shopify Blog

- ecommerceFuel

Specialize

Most successful dropshipping businesses specialize in a single niche or product. Do not just sell backpacks; sell backpacks specially designed for bow hunters. Narrowing down helps you stand out and you can barely go wrong with it.

Long-Term Perspective

A dropshipping store, like all other businesses, requires great investment and commitment. You cannot build a lucrative stream of passive income in a few months. In fact, the first few months will not be easy. You will face so many obstacles and you must be mentally prepared.

Outstanding Service

In this era of social media, the best thing you can do for your business is making your customers happy. Treat them badly and they will announce it to the world. Treat them well and they may do the same.

Do not Get Stuck on Details

Your business' theme, logo, or name are not the determinants of your success. The above five factors are what matter the most. The most difficult and important step is building the business. If you have everything set and you are serious about this, start now. Ecommerce is growing at a rapid pace. Every entrepreneur and business are trying to use digital salesmanship to make money, one way or another. Some ecommerce strategies will give you better results than others. Dropshipping is one of the tactics that are less popular than they were some time back. This can be attributed to new constraints that have rendered it less profitable. 2019 is a confusing and disruptive year. It is a good time to ask whether dropshipping is still a profitable venture or not. Dropshipping, like any other business venture, will only succeed if you make your customers a top priority. Many newbies think that dropshipping is an effective way of making easy and quick money. On the contrary, it is a complicated process and you must be constantly on your toes. While your work is made easier because you do not have to stock goods, this creates a new set of challenges (think ensuring customers' satisfaction and issuing refunds). Many people who dived into dropshipping thinking that is a quick way to attain business success realized that they were mistaken, and they suffered the consequences. There are good ecommerce veterans that will truthfully tell you what mistakes they made while starting out. However, some beginners will still ignore the advice and fall into the same pit. A great number of them fail to understand the essentials needed to make this venture successful. Some of the obstacles you will face involve quality control and high shipping costs. Contrary to popular belief, dropshipping is not quite secure. Neither you nor your customers will be interacting with the supplier face to face and this makes it easy for you to get scammed. A supplier can also deliver low quality goods to your customers causing dissatisfaction and irritation. Due to this, you must get dropshipping training first and look for trustworthy suppliers. They are not easy to find, and they can be expensive too. However, a supplier can be the reason your business fails or succeeds. Do not let suppliers lure you with lower prices. Do your due diligence and make sure they can be trusted first. It is better to have happy repeat customers than one-time angry ones. The dropshipping model requires extra homework on your end. You or your workers should be constantly researching to find new engagement models, products, and suppliers. There are aspects of dropshipping that you can only prepare yourself for. Quality control, for instance, is out of your hands. You will just have to come up with a way to make sure that your customers get what they pay for. Efficient customer care is also crucial. Although the challenges are many, some entrepreneurs still try out dropshipping because the startup costs are low. If you are keen enough, do your research and master the industry, you will be immensely successful.

When shoppers are visiting a new online store, they look for customer reviews. They want to know whether they will have a great experience. But what if your store is completely new, you have not made any sales and, therefore, have no reviews? How do you get customers to trust you and make purchases? This is a problem that every entrepreneur must face. Fortunately for you, there is something you can do about it. The nine strategies outlined below will help you win the trust of potential customers. Consumers barely trust brands—they are all out to make money. However, they easily trust people. Introduce the person behind your online store. This tactic works even better if you make your own products. The About Us page is the perfect space for this. Focus more on yourself and less on your product. Content helps you connect with new users. It offers a perfect chance to introduce yourself. Regular blogging shows that you care about your business and customers. Content also allows consumers to familiarize themselves with your brand and your voice. Even as you try to show customers that they can trust your business, your site should also look trustworthy. With cyber security being a huge issue, customers do not easily give out their financial information. A good return policy shows that the customer experience is important to you and you are confident about what you sell. People are more likely to buy if they are assured, they can return the item if they do not like it. When customers are confused, they may try to contact you through social media, email, or your contact form. Be available and answer their questions quickly and clearly. The chances of making a sale increase when customers know more about the product. Here are some things that you may want to add to your descriptions:

- Detailed measurements of the product
- Exact weight of your product
- Manufacturing materials or ingredients
- Warranty information
- Specific product features

Product samples may make people more interested in your store and they also inspire trust. This method may not be applicable to all businesses. Consider giving the samples to a specific number of people then ask for reviews. Alternatively, send the items to bloggers or influencers who will, in turn, help you reach your target audience. An FAQ page is instrumental in answering user questions. Through the page, you can explain how you run the store, offer product information, demonstrate your knowledge and give more information about your products and brand. Preview your store both on mobile and desktop to see how the experience is like from the homepage to checkout. Take care of any mistakes, even the small ones.